1001 TIPS FOR SUCCESSFUL GARDENING

1001 TIPS FOR SUCCESSFUL GARDENING

Sharon Graham

Illustrations by Karen Howitt

E. P. DUTTON, INC.   **NEW YORK**

Published in the United States by E. P. Dutton, Inc., 2 Park Avenue,
New York, N.Y. 10016

Library of Congress Cataloging in Publication Data

Graham, Sharon
    1001 tips for successful gardening.
    1. Gardening. I. Title. II. Title: One thousand one
tips for successful gardening. III. Title: One thousand
and one tips for successful gardening.
SB451.G67   1983   635   82-21064

ISBN: 0-525-93278-X

DESIGNED BY EARL TIDWELL

10 9 8 7 6 5 4 3 2 1

First Edition

To my husband

Contents

Introduction

Gardening has become America's number one hobby. Like most pleasurable pastimes, gardening can be addictive, but don't worry; this is one habit you needn't try to break. Gardening is good for you physically and mentally. The satisfaction derived from discovering a new leaf, shoot or bud emerging from a favorite plant can't be measured.

Working with plants is a pleasure, but for success it does take some know-how. If you think you have bad luck with plants, luck is not your problem, but lack of knowledge. Subscribe to a garden magazine, borrow garden books from the library, read them and try their suggestions. Gardening experts don't always agree, so use the books as a guideline, but don't be afraid to try your own ideas. If you experience a failure, that merely means you now know how not to do it the next time.

You don't need ten acres in the country to be a gardener. If you have ten acres, that is great, but even an apartment dweller can have a window garden or a garden under lights and know the pleasures of gardening.

Even though it is pleasurable, gardening can be hard work. This book contains tips to help keep the work to a minimum and make the growing easy. Since most plants start as seeds and seedlings, so will we.

1001 TIPS FOR SUCCESSFUL GARDENING

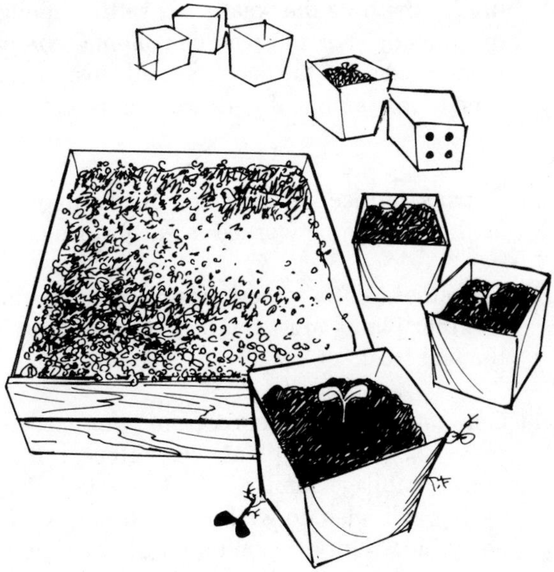

1

Seeds and Seedlings

Testing last year's seeds

To avoid disappointment when planting seeds left over from last year's garden, test them first. Here's how: Sprinkle a dozen or so on a moist paper towel, roll it up and place it in a plastic bag, close the bag and put it in a warm place for a few days. If more than two-thirds of the seeds sprout, plant as usual. If less than two-thirds sprout, either discard the seeds or plant them thickly. If less than half sprout, pitch them and buy new seeds.

The right time to sow

Don't start your seeds indoors too soon. Because of short, dark days, seeds sown in January or February will probably not get enough light, and so plants will be tall, weak and spindly by the time the weather is settled enough for transplanting outside. For most garden plants, count back six weeks from the date of the last expected frost in your area and plant then. For example, if your frost date is May 15, plant at about April 1.

❧ Carrots, lettuce, radishes and onions may be planted as soon as the soil can be worked in early spring.

❧ Tomatoes, corn, green beans, peppers and other warm-weather plants must not be planted in the garden until after the last frost.

❧ Get continued production from your garden by second cropping. Cool-weather plants like lettuce, radishes and members of the cabbage family, which are usually planted in early spring, will also do well in fall, if planted in late summer or early fall. Plant a second crop of tomatoes in midsummer to come on when the first planting diminishes. Corn and beans can be planted for a long period during the summer for an extended harvest. Check with your county extension agent for planting dates in your area.

❧ Here's an easy way to find the latest planting date for your fall garden. Add seven to the number of days required for maturity, as listed on the seed packet of the vegetables you wish to grow. Then find the first expected date of frost in your area and count backward that number of days.

Getting an early start

❧ Try sowing some lettuce in late fall for extra early lettuce next spring.

Getting a late start

❧ Turnips planted in the fall have a better flavor than those planted in the spring because the frost makes them sweeter. Plant six to eight weeks before the first expected frost for an early winter harvest.

Homemade containers for starting seeds

❦ Use plastic milk jugs as containers for starting seeds. Just cut off the top and poke drain holes in the bottom if you will be planting only a few seeds. If you have more seeds to plant, lay the jug on its side and cut off the top side, leaving the handle and lid in place. Poke holes in the opposite side. Fill with soil and sow the seeds. Remember, starter pots should be clean to prevent disease.

Containers for seeds that resist transplanting

❦ Styrofoam drinking cups make great little seed starter pots. Poke a pencil through the bottom to make a drain hole. Fill with potting soil or other medium. Place several in a tray or shallow pan for easier handling. When the seedlings are ready to be transplanted, peel the cups off without disturbing the tender roots.

❦ Individual peat pots are also handy for plants that resist transplanting. When it is time to transplant, peel off as much of the pot as possible. Make sure the entire pot is buried, for any left exposed will act as a wick, drawing moisture from the soil around the plant's roots.

❦ The easiest starter pots to use are Jiffy 7s or Jiffy 9s—compressed peat pellets that expand when you soak them in a pan of warm water. When they are fully expanded, drop one or two seeds into each and set in flats or trays in a sunny window. Don't let them dry out. If you planted two seeds in each, cut off the weakest plant so that only one healthy seedling remains in each pellet. When you transplant outside, tear off the netting that surrounds the pellet to allow for better root growth, and plant the pellet directly in the garden.

A clean planting medium for healthy plants

❦ The easiest way to ensure clean medium is to buy bags of vermiculite, chopped sphagnum, potting soil or soilless mix. If you want to use garden soil in your mixture, sterilize it in the oven first. Put it in a shallow baking pan, moisten, and

3

bake at 180° F. for two hours. Never use garden soil alone; it does not drain well enough.

A rule of thumb for how deep to plant

A general rule in sowing seeds is to cover them to twice the depth of their diameter. A seed one-fourth inch in diameter should be covered with one-half inch of soil. Don't, whatever you do, bury seeds too deeply or they won't come up at all. Very fine seeds such as petunia, begonia and gloxinia do not need to be covered with soil at all, but you should cover the containers with plastic so they won't dry out.

Planting tiny seeds

Sowing tiny seeds such as petunias thinly is difficult. To make the job easier, mix the seeds with dry sand before sowing.

Containing disease in containers

Plant your seeds in containers in rows. If disease strikes, it will go down the row, leaf to leaf, but it will stop at the end of the row. If seeds are broadcast, the whole container is likely to be infected.

Two crops from one sowing

Beet seeds are actually tiny fruits containing several seeds. For this reason, you will need to thin your beet row when the young plants appear. Thin plants in the row to about three inches apart and cook the thinnings to serve as greens. Delicious.

What is it?

To avoid confusion, always label pots or flats of seeds, telling the variety and the date planted.

Cut washed Styrofoam trays from meat packages into three-fourth-inch strips, across the width of the trays, to use as plant labels. Use a ballpoint pen or a permanent felt-tip pen to write on them.

Do not disturb

- To water flats of seeds without disturbing them or washing them out, use a plastic squeeze bottle, such as a dish detergent bottle, and squeeze gently.

- Another watering technique that will not disturb seeds: Set a newly planted seed container in a pan of lukewarm water. The water will soak into the potting soil through the drain holes, providing the necessary moisture.

Providing a humid climate

- Insert seed trays in clear plastic bags to hold in humidity and to reduce the need to water. High humidity speeds germination greatly, but also promotes growth of mold, so check the trays daily. If mold begins to form, open the bags and let the fresh air inside.

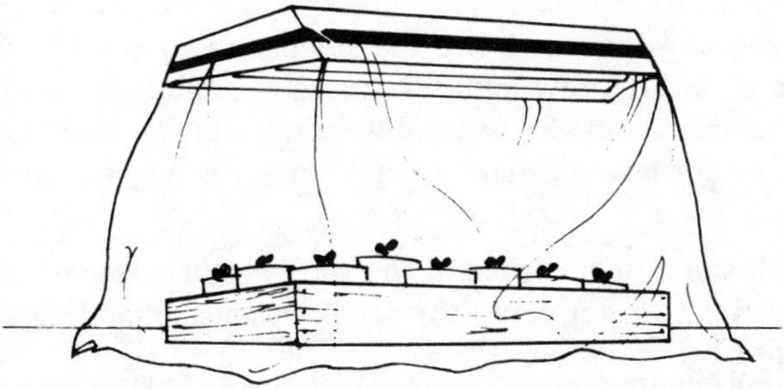

- When starting seeds under fluorescent lights, you'll find they germinate more quickly and evenly if you make a tent to hold in the humidity. Tape a sheet of plastic around the rim of the reflector, and let it hang down to touch the table where the flats are sitting. Fluorescent bulbs do not get hot, so there is no danger of fire.

Some seeds like it warm

- Place a planted flat on an electrically heated serving tray to provide even heat.

✿ Another method for keeping seeded flats warm is to place them on top of your water heater or your refrigerator if the motor is in the top. Cover with clear plastic to keep the flats from drying out.

✿ An electric heating cable would be a worthwhile investment if you start garden plants or bedding plants from seed each year. Since it is waterproof, it can be placed in the bottom of the seed flat or on a table with the flat sitting on top. You can also use the heating cable to warm the soil of a cold frame, so your plants will have a head start in spring.

Speeding germination

✿ To speed germination of seeds that have a thick hard seed coat, such as lotus or banana, use a file to make a notch in the coat so the seed can absorb water more quickly. Be careful not to damage the inner parts of the seeds.

✿ If you find that seeds are too small to hold and file, you can run them for a few minutes in a rock tumbler with a handful of coarse sand. Rock tumblers are usually used to polish stones for jewelry making but come in handy for this too.

✿ Chill snapdragon seeds in the refrigerator a few days before planting. Do not cover the seeds because snapdragons need light to germinate.

✿ To make peanuts germinate faster, remove the outer shells but leave the red skins on. Soak the seeds overnight before planting. Sprinkle the planted row with peanut inoculant in water.

✿ To make sure tiny seeds such as carrots or petunias germinate well and don't dry out when planted directly in the garden, sow the seeds about one-half inch deep and then cover the row with a layer of clear plastic. The plastic holds the moisture in and, if it rains, keeps the seeds from being washed away. Remove the plastic as soon as seedlings appear.

Transplanting the seedlings

❀ Most seedlings are ready for transplanting from their original containers when they have at least one set of true leaves (usually there is also one set of seed leaves).

❀ Because seedlings are very fragile, when you transplant them, always handle them by a leaf, rather than by the stem. A leaf can be replaced, but a damaged stem can be fatal.

❀ To separate crowded seedlings for transplanting, dig up a clump and drop them on the potting bench. In this way they will separate with less damage than if they were pulled apart.

❀ When setting out transplants, water each plant as you plant it. If you wait until after planting them all, the roots of the first ones planted may dry out.

❀ Do your transplanting on a cloudy day if possible. Plants set out on a hot sunny day will probably wilt.

Getting ready to move

❀ Young plants should be hardened off (adjusted to outdoor conditions) before they are transplanted to the garden. This is done over a period of several days. Begin on a warm sunny day that is not too windy. Set the plants outside in a *shady* spot for about two hours. The next day, put them out for four hours. Each day leave them out two or three hours longer, shifting them gradually to a sunnier spot. On the fifth day or so, they should be strong enough to be planted outside.

Temporary help for new plants

❀ Tender young plants need protection from sun and wind the first few days after being transplanted outdoors. Take a heavy piece of cardboard and shove it into the soil, slanted toward the plant, on the sunny side of the plant. Leave this in place until the plant is sturdy enough to survive on its own.

❀ Cut the bottoms from milk jugs or cereal boxes and put them over young plants to protect them from cold nights in early spring.

Mark your row

❀ Use radishes as row markers for slow-germinating crops. Plant a few radish seeds in the same row with the other seeds, and you can tell exactly where the row is, and avoid hoeing it out.

❀ Mark all rows as you plant them. If you're an experienced gardener, you don't really need named labels (you'll recognize them when they come up), but use a bare stick at each end of the row to locate it.

Starting sweet potatoes

❀ Start your own sweet potato plants. One month before your last expected frost date, plant one seed sweet potato per six-inch pot, in sandy soil. Keep in a warm sunny window. When it is time to set them out in the garden, just pull up the sprouts and transplant them. There should be several in each pot.

Saving seeds from your own garden

❀ Don't save seeds from hybrid plants—always keep seed packets of what you plant in the spring in order to identify which are hybrids. Because hybrid seeds are produced by carefully-controlled cross-pollination, they do not breed true. But do save seeds from nonhybrid plants because these usually produce new plants that are true to parent plants.

❀ To save seeds, wait until flowers or seed pods are completely dry before you collect them. For plants with very fine seeds, cut off the entire flower head or pod rather than casually breaking them off. Break pods open over newspaper or into a paperbag. Let the seeds dry a few more days for good measure and then store as directed below.

Store seeds properly

❀ Many kinds of seeds will remain viable for several years if stored properly. Place in a glass jar; add a small cloth bag full of calcined clay (kitty litter) to the jar (use the plain, not the green or scented kind). The clay absorbs moisture and prevents mold. Now close the jar tightly and keep it in the refrigerator or in some other cool place.

2
Vegetables

Where to locate your garden

❀ Plant your garden where it will get at least six hours of sun each day. Full sun is even better. If you're planning in January, don't forget about shade trees that may block sun when in full leaf.

❀ For your convenience, plant the garden as close to the house as possible. This will also help discourage raids by hungry animals.

Where not to locate your garden

❀ Don't plant your garden in a low spot. Vegetables need soil with good drainage, and frost settles in low areas.

❀ Don't plant your garden near black walnut trees. These trees produce juglone from their roots and leaves, and juglone is toxic to tomatoes, potatoes, and other vegetables.

❀ Any large tree near a garden will sap it of nutrients and moisture, so it's best to avoid planting near trees.

Small is beautiful

❀ Think small when planning your garden. Just remember that a small well-kept garden will produce many more vegetables than a large neglected one. Also, a small, manageable garden is a pleasure—especially for beginners and busy people—but a large garden can be an overwhelming chore.

Space-saving ideas

❀ Save garden space by planting bush pumpkins. They need only one-third the space taken by vining pumpkins.

❀ Sweet corn and pole beans make good garden companions. Plant them in the same row and let the beans climb up the cornstalks. The beans pay for their support by providing nitrogen in the soil for the corn.

❀ Another garden space-saver is to plant radishes and lettuce in the sweet corn rows. These quick-to-grow crops will be harvested before the corn needs the space.

Support hose

❀ Use strips of worn-out pantyhose to tie plants to supporting stakes. The nylon strips are strong enough to do the job, yet stretchy and soft enough that they won't damage the plants.

Get an early start

❀ You can get an early start with your tender garden plants if you have a way to protect them from frost and cool spring winds. Form a length of concrete reinforcing wire into an arch and place it over the row of young plants. Cover the wire with clear plastic. Fasten it down to the ground with stakes to keep it in place during windy days.

Compost without a compost pile

❀ If you don't want to make a compost pile, just bury kitchen refuse in between the rows in your garden. It takes only a few minutes each day or so, and is good for the soil and plants. You can also bury weeds, leaves and other organic trash, but be sure the weeds haven't formed seeds. Also, let them lie in the sun a few days to die, so you will be burying rather than replanting them.

ASPARAGUS

The best place to plant

❀ Since asparagus is a perennial it has to be planted where it will not be disturbed from year to year. For plump healthy asparagus, an ideal location is at the back of a flower bed. The asparagus plants will benefit from the cultivation, feeding and watering you give the flowers, while the ferny growth of the mature asparagus makes a beautiful background for your flowers.

Getting the bed established

❀ Many asparagus beds last as long as twenty to twenty-five years, so it is well worth the trouble to get your bed well established. Here's how you do it: Dig a trench a foot deep and half fill with a mixture of soil and rotted manure. Place the crowns in the trench, twelve inches apart. Cover with three inches of soil. Water well. Fill the trench gradually with soil through the summer as the asparagus grows. It should be filled by the end of August.

When to harvest

❀ Don't harvest a new asparagus bed until the third year after planting. If harvested too soon, the plants will be permanently weakened. It may seem like a long wait, but when you consider that your bed is going to be around for twenty-five years or more, it's worth it.

❀ Asparagus is ready to cut when the spears are six to eight inches tall.

- Harvest asparagus through early summer, then let the ferny stalks mature to manufacture the food needed to produce a good yield the following spring.

The right food for healthy plants

- To assure a better crop next spring, add a four-inch rotted manure mulch (do not use fresh manure) to asparagus in the summer. Asparagus is a heavy feeder.

A great place to grow tomatoes

- Asparagus roots kill nematodes, so the asparagus bed is a good spot to plant a few tomatoes, which are often attacked by these pests. Put a tomato plant in any thin spot and watch it produce.

Don't waste it

- Don't throw away asparagus that has grown tough. Cut off the tender tips and cook these as usual. Then, run the tough ends through the blender and use the pulp to make delicious cream of asparagus soup. If you don't have a blender, simply chop up the tough stalks when raw and cook the soup, then purée it in a food mill.

BEANS

Pick them early or late

- For tender snap beans, pick them when the pods are just beginning to fill out, or even before. For shelled beans, such as limas, let the beans mature.

Take it easy

- Don't break your back picking bunch beans. Take a bucket along to sit on. Pick two rows at once, sitting between them. You will be able to pick a lot of beans before it is even necessary to move the bucket.

Grow some sprouts

- Grow some mung bean sprouts to add to an Oriental dish or to add extra crunch to a salad. Seeds are available from many mail-order seed companies. Put about one-fourth cup of the seeds in a glass or plastic bowl. Cover with water and soak overnight. Drain and cover with a damp paper towel. Put in a dark place such as inside a cabinet. That evening, cover with water and soak overnight again. Repeat the procedure of draining, covering with a damp paper towel, etc. Do this each day until the beans sprout. When you see tiny leaves forming, they are ready to eat. Either use them immediately or refrigerate until you are ready to use them.

BEETS

- Beets are at their best when about two inches in diameter or a bit smaller. Harvest them when they are still young and tender because they get tougher as they get larger and older.

CABBAGE

Slow them down

- If you have a lot of cabbages that are going to be ready at the same time, and want to slow the growth of some of them, all you have to do is twist the head a half-turn. This is a simplified method of root pruning. It breaks loose the smaller roots, slowing growth, but the tap root is left intact so that the plant will slowly mature.

- Cut when the heads feel firm. If allowed to grow too long, the cabbage will split.

Keep them coming

- For a second cabbage crop, cut off the first mature head, leaving the rest of the plant in place. Several small heads will form around the cut edge. They will be quite small, but good.

CARROTS

Help them come up and grow straight

- Plant radishes in the same row with your carrots. The fast-growing radishes will break through the soil first, making it easier for the carrots to follow. The radishes will be harvested long before the carrots need the space.

❧ Branching carrots are usually caused by their efforts to break through hard soil. To avoid this condition, keep the soil well cultivated.

CAULIFLOWER AND CELERY
Blanching the easy way

❧ Clip cauliflower leaves together with clothespins to blanch the heads.

❧ When celery plants are about 12 inches tall, slip a six-inch diameter drain tile over each plant to blanch it.

CORN
When and where to plant

❧ Sweet corn will recover from mild frosts. If it is a warm spring, it is worth the risk to plant early, since this will give the corn a head start before the hot dry weather of summer. If it is a cold wet spring, forget about planting until later. The seeds won't germinate well; most will rot. Those that grow will be passed up by later plantings.

❧ Sweet corn is wind-pollinated. The pollen from the tassels must fall on the silks for good full ears of corn. To help promote good pollination, plant sweet corn in short blocks of at least four rows, rather than one or two long rows.

❧ Don't plant the newer super-sweet varieties of corn near ordinary sweet corn. It will probably cross-pollinate and lose much of its sweetness.

Suckers help

❧ There is no need to remove suckers from your corn plants. They can be helpful to the plant in dry weather, and breaking them off provides an easy entryway for disease.

Harvesting

❧ The sugar in sweet corn changes to starch rather quickly after the corn is picked. For the sweetest, best-tasting corn, put a pot of water on to heat up as you go out to pick the corn. Bring the shucked ears in and put them in the boiling water as soon as possible.

❧ To pick the best, feel the ends of sweet corn ears when the silks are brown. If the ears are rounded, they are ready. If the ears are pointed, wait a while till they fill out more.

CUCUMBERS

Mulch under cucumber (and pumpkin and squash) vines

❧ If your cucumber vines sprawl on the ground, save a lot of work by mulching under the vines with several layers of newspaper, topped by a layer of aluminum foil. The mulch conserves moisture, smothers weeds, and keeps the fruit from touching damp soil, which in turn helps to prevent rot and insect damage. The foil deters certain insects.

Prevent bitterness

❧ Keep cucumbers well watered during prolonged dry spells to prevent bitterness.

❧ Bitterness can also be caused by soil deficiency. Add lime at planting time as a preventive measure.

Grow them straight

❧ If you want straight cukes, grow them on a fence or trellis. Gravity makes them straight.

Save space with trellises

❧ Save garden space by planting cucumbers and other vining plants along the garden fence. Train them to grow up the fence.

❧ Make a tower trellis out of concrete reinforcing wire to support vigorous vining plants such as cucumbers (and muskmelons). Use bolt cutters to cut the heavy wire, form a large cylinder and wire the ends together. Set it in the garden and plant the vines around its perimeter.

❧ A good trellis for vining plants can be made from a wooden, expanding baby gate. Just hang it vertically from a post or horizontally with a post at each end.

Grow a weird one

❧ This is just for fun. When you see a tiny cucumber beginning to form on the vine, slip it into a small, odd-shaped clear plastic bottle. When the cuke has grown till it fills the bottle, remove it from the vine and carefully cut away the bottle. You will have a unique cucumber.

Keep them coming

❧ Keep large cucumbers picked to keep up production. Even one mature cuke on the vine will greatly reduce production of fruit.

EGGPLANT
Start with seeds

❧ Eggplant is best started from seeds sown directly in the garden. Plants sold at garden centers in cellpaks are usually rootbound and go into shock when transplanted.

❧ For the best-tasting eggplant, pick the fruit when it is only half-grown. If allowed to mature, it may become bitter.

GOURDS
Don't pick too soon

❧ Wait till frost kills the vines to harvest gourds and pumpkins.

KOHLRABI
A radish replacement

❧ If you like radishes but can't eat them, try growing kohlrabi as a crisp, mild-flavored substitute. Like radishes, kohlrabi can be planted in early spring, as soon as the soil can be worked. The part that is eaten is above the soil level, a swelled part of the stem commonly called a bulb. This is delicious when peeled, sliced and eaten raw, but is equally good cooked.

❧ Use kohlrabi when the bulb is about two and one-half inches in diameter for the best flavor. If allowed to grow larger than this, the bulb will be tough.

LETTUCE
Plant early or late

❧ Lettuce bolts (goes to seed) quickly in hot, dry weather. Avoid this problem by planting early, as soon as the soil can be worked, or in fall to take advantage of the cool weather. Water during dry spells.

❧ For tasty, attractive salads, plant several varieties of lettuce in the same row. Include the appealing red-leaf Ruby lettuce.

❧ Cut when the heads feel firm. If allowed to grow too long, the lettuce may rot or bolt.

Making leaf lettuce last

❧ For continued production, pick the outside leaves of loose-leaf lettuce (this also works with spinach and chard). New leaves will sprout from the center of the plant.

MELONS
Fertilize and water all at once

❧ To grow healthy melons, as you make the planting hills, sink a six-inch or larger flower pot in the center of each hill. Fill the pot half-full of manure. When you water the plants, pour the water in the pot. It will seep into the soil through the pot's drain hole, fertilizing the plants at the same time.

Support the fruit

❀ Muskmelons or cantaloupes grown on a trellis or fence will need support as the fruits grow. You can make a handy sling for each melon from old nylon hose. Tie the sling to the fence and place the melon in it.

❀ Keep your melons from rotting on the vine before they ripen. Use the bottom half of a foam egg carton. Poke a drain hole in each egg cup, then place the carton under a melon. The carton keeps the melon from touching the moist soil, which helps prevent rot as well as insect damage.

❀ If you don't have enough egg cartons, set the melons on bricks.

Speed up ripening

❀ The fruit will mature more quickly if you pinch out the tips of each melon vine after it has set about three fruits.

You can tell they are ripe

❀ You will know your muskmelons are ripe and ready to pick when they have a crack at the base of the stem, when they are slightly soft and when they have a delicious fragrance.

❀ Watermelons are ready when the tendril nearest the melon turns brown, and the underside of the melon is a creamy white color.

OKRA

❀ Okra is best when the pods are small. If you have too many to use, pick them anyway, even if you must throw them away. Pods left to mature on the plants will greatly diminish production.

ONIONS

Keep them in place

❀ If cats or squirrels scatter your onion sets from the row, just lay a board over each row until onions are securely rooted, then remove the board. Believe it or not, even earthworms (the big nightcrawlers) will upend onion sets. They pull the nose end of the set into an opening of their burrows. The board trick also stops the worms from rearranging your sets.

Grow good, big onions

❀ Don't smother your onions with soil if you want them to grow big. Push sets firmly into loose soil, but don't cover. As they grow, leave only enough soil around them to cover the roots.

❀ When seeds form on your onion plants, break off the seeds and seed stalk. If these are left on the plant, it will become woody right down through the onion bulb.

❀ When onion tops fall over, it is a signal that the bulbs are ready for harvesting. Never pull onions; dig them. Pulling can bruise the stems and cause rot. After digging, allow them to air dry in a frostfree place for a few days before storing.

Have green onions in winter

❀ Before using an onion during the winter, core it, leaving the roots on the end of the core. Plant the core in a pot of soil, water it, and set in a sunny window. It will soon sprout tender green shoots that you can snip and use in salads or to add flavor to cooked dishes.

PEAS
Grow edible-pod peas for a many-splendored vegetable

❀ Sugar Snap peas, which have edible pods, are a wonderfully versatile vegetable. Deliciously sweet and crunchy, they are great raw in salads, delectable stir-fried with mushrooms and garlic, and good snapped and steamed like green beans. Or you can let them mature, then shell and eat them like ordinary peas. Plants grow up to six feet tall and more, and need a support to climb on, but they are worth the trouble, for they keep producing for weeks, if you keep them picked. Stop picking and they will stop producing.

19

To eat the pods of sugar peas, pick them while they are still flat and small. To shell, let the pods fill out, but pick before the pods start to dry.

Free fertilizer from the roots of peas

The roots of peas and other legumes add nitrogen to the soil, so when peas are through producing, cut plants off instead of pulling them up. The soil will get the full benefit of their nitrogen-producing abilities.

PEPPERS
They can be self-supporting

The stems of pepper plants are rather brittle. If you don't stake your peppers, try planting them two together for more strength. The wind will be less likely to break them when they are heavy with fruit when there are two stalks instead of only one.

POPCORN

Do not plant popcorn near sweet corn, or it will cross-pollinate and ruin the quality of both the popcorn and the sweet corn.

How to shell it

After you've dried the ears of popcorn, you can shell them easily, without getting sore hands, by simply rubbing two ears together. Hold them over a large pan to catch the grains as they fall.

POTATOES
Grow them the easy way

Don't break off the long sprouts that grow on seed potatoes. Leave them on the seed pieces and plant so that the shoots are vertical. Your potatoes will be off to a head start.

The easiest potato-growing method I know is to lay the pieces of seed potato, with at least one eye to each piece, on the soil, and press lightly, using a hoe or your foot. Do not cover with soil. Cover with a six-inch layer of straw. The straw will act as a mulch, conserving moisture and smothering weeds, but the potato plants will come up through the straw. When it is time to harvest the crop, remove the straw. The potatoes can simply be picked up. No digging necessary!

❀ You can dig a few new potatoes when the plants start to bloom, but for the main crop, wait till the plants start to die.

Keep potato plants healthy

❀ Save wood ashes to add to the potato patch. The ashes are a good source of potash.

❀ Help prevent disease in potatoes and related plants. Potatoes, tomatoes, peppers and strawberries all share some of the same diseases. If planted in the same area year after year, the disease organisms build up in the soil. If possible, plant in a different area and rotate yearly (except for strawberries) with other crops.

Keep the green away

❀ Green skin on potatoes means that sunlight is reaching them. To prevent this condition, which causes bitterness and is also toxic, pile more soil over the hills or add a thick mulch of straw.

Saving the vitamins

❀ If you peel potatoes, you are losing a lot of the vitamins and minerals, not to mention valuable time. Potatoes with the skins on are good boiled, baked, sautéed or fried.

Try this unusual mixture

❀ Seeded cucumbers and onions make a delicious addition to fried potatoes. Slice one small onion and equal portions of cucumbers and potatoes. Fry in sesame oil or peanut oil for a tasty and easy supper dish.

PUMPKINS
Grow them big

❧ To grow the largest pumpkin or melon, first choose a large variety, keep the plants watered during dry weather, and then remove all but the largest, healthiest looking fruit on each vine. The vine will then put all its effort into one large fruit rather then dividing it among several smaller ones.

Eat the blooms

❧ Did you know you can eat pumpkin and squash blossoms? For an unusual taste treat, pick the blossoms when they open, rinse and inspect for insects. Drain on a paper towel, then dip in pancake batter and fry till golden brown . . . Delicious!

Cook pumpkins the easy way

❧ The easiest way to prepare a pumpkin for pies is to bake it. Stab a few holes in the top to keep it from exploding, and place it in a baking pan in case some of the juice leaks. Bake at 375° F. until it is tender. This will take an hour or more, depending upon the size of the pumpkin. Let it cool. Remove the seeds, then peel, cut in chunks and purée in the blender. It peels so much easier than a raw pumpkin . . . no more cut hands.

RHUBARB
Add new life to old rhubarb

❧ Rhubarb plantings that have been growing for four or five years may need a boost. Dig a trench beside the plants and fill it with compost and well-rotted manure. Water during dry weather.

Use rhubarb to stretch fruits

❧ Most people know about adding rhubarb to strawberry pies, but did you know that it also makes delicious jams in combination with other fruits? Substitute rhubarb for half of whatever other fruit is called for in the recipe. It combines especially well with strawberries or raspberries.

SQUASH
Get an early start

❀ For early squash (and melons), start indoors in pots. Because squash cannot stand to be rootbound, plant them in four-inch or larger pots, one seed per pot.

Grow spaghetti

❀ If you have plenty of garden space, grow some of the novelty spaghetti squash. Three plants will produce plenty for a family of four, and some for your neighbors, too. When the fruit is about eight inches long, pick and cut in half lengthwise. Remove the seeds and boil the squash for 20 minutes. Drain; scrape out the fibers with a fork. Serve with spaghetti sauce (try pesto, made from your basil, as well as tomato sauces) or just butter and salt for a tasty dish.

SWISS CHARD

❀ If Swiss chard gets ahead of you and gets too large, just cut it down to about four inches above ground level. It will soon send up tender new leaves.

❀ For extra-early spring greens, heavily mulch Swiss chard in early winter and it should survive to provide a green treat when you are most anxious for it.

TOMATOES
What kind to plant

❀ The best way to avoid problems is to buy disease-resistant plants. If your tomatoes did poorly last summer in spite of good growing conditions, plenty of water and a regular feeding program, they were probably victims of disease. The disease-resistant plants will be tagged VFNT, if they are resistant to all four diseases: verticillium wilt, fusarium wilt, nematodes (not a disease, really, but tiny worms), and tobacco mosaic.

❀ Plant determinate tomatoes if you want your tomato crop to ripen nearly all at once, which makes it handy for canning and freezing. Plant indeterminate tomatoes if you want an extended season.

Spindly plants will do

❀ Stocky plants are better, but don't despair if you can find only spindly tomato plants when buying plants for your garden. When transplanting them to the garden, remove the lower leaves and bury all but the top one-third of the plant. The buried stem will produce roots along its entire length, resulting in a sturdy plant.

New beds for your tomato plants

❀ If you want to grow healthy tomatoes, change the location of the tomato garden from year to year. Tomatoes grown in the same spot every year will deplete the soil of magnesium, and also increase the likelihood of diseases. Magnesium deficiency may cause blossom drop, resulting in poor fruit production. If you have a space problem, and must plant in the same spot, choose wilt-resistant varieties, and add one-fourth cup of epsom salts to the soil around each plant. Epsom salts consists of magnesium sulfate, which will improve the soil.

❀ Protect tender tomato plants set out in early summer from cold and wind damage. Use a wire tomato cage around the plants, and wrap the cage in clear plastic. Clear plastic lets the warmth and light of the sun in, but keeps cold wind away from the plants.

❀ Dry weather and a calcium deficiency in the soil can cause blossom-end rot on tomatoes. Prevent this by adding dolomitic lime to the soil, watering during dry spells and using a thick mulch to preserve soil moisture.

❀ Tomato blossom drop is often caused by very hot weather, but another cause can be too much nitrogen in the soil. Tomatoes need a low nitrogen fertilizer such as 5-10-10 to set fruit.

❀ Unstaked tomatoes are usually damaged by sunburn. Prevent this by leaning old window screens over them, from the sunny side.

Get more tomatoes

❧ Caged tomatoes produce more fruit that is easier to pick, and will have fewer rotted fruits. They also need less space in the garden. Make cages from woven wire fencing, sold at farm supply stores. Cut the fence into pieces at least five feet long or longer. Form each piece into a cylinder and fasten the ends together with wire. Set a cylinder on end over each tomato plant and anchor it down with stakes to prevent its toppling in the wind. Caged tomatoes should be four feet apart each way for easy harvesting.

❧ You can start new tomato plants from suckers. Suckers look like miniature plants growing from the main stem at the leaf axils. Snap them off and stick in moist clean sand or coarse vermiculite. Place in a spot protected from direct sun until they have rooted. Transplant to the garden and you will have a second crop when your first tomatoes are slowing production.

Eat tomatoes all year

❧ You can have tomatoes year-round if you grow them indoors in containers during the winter. Choose dwarfs such as Patio or Pixie. Plant in sterile potting medium, the first planting in August, for fruit in November. Transplant to one gallon containers and feed with 5-10-10 fertilizer every two weeks. To pollinate the blooms, dab each with a soft paintbrush such as artists use.

Good ways to use them

❧ For a delicious and unusual salad that makes its own dressing, try Great-Grandma Moffett's celery and tomato salad. Cut ripe red tomatoes into bite-size chunks. Add several ribs of celery that have been cut into slices. Sprinkle with about a tablespoon of sugar per medium-size bowl of salad, add salt and pepper and stir to mix. Although sugar with tomatoes sounds awful, this is really great.

❧ If you can't wait for your tomatoes to ripen, try frying some green tomatoes. Just slice, dip in flour, or a mixture of flour and cornmeal, sprinkle with salt, and fry in a little bacon grease or butter till tender.

❧ Green tomato relish is a good way to save the ones that would be ruined by the first hard freeze. Coarsely grind vegetables to make four cups of green tomatoes, four cups of cucumbers, four cups of sweet red, yellow or green peppers (use all three if you have them, for a very pretty relish) and one cup of onions. Dissolve one-half cup of salt in eight cups of water. Pour over the vegetables and let stand four hours. Drain, then cover with water, and drain again. Add two teaspoons each of cinnamon, cloves and allspice to four cups of vinegar and one and a half cups of brown sugar. Heat to a boil and pour over the vegetables. Let stand overnight. Simmer till hot through, bringing to a boil. Put in jars and seal. Makes seven to eight pints. This recipe can be adjusted according to what vegetables you may have. You can use carrots, zucchini or cabbage, and it is okay to change the proportions of the vegetables, as long as they total twelve cups plus the one cup of onions.

ZUCCHINI

❧ Pick when the squash are about eight inches long. They can be used when larger, but small ones are more tender, and you will have plenty, for they are very prolific.

3

Fruits
and Berries

Be fruitful and multiply

❀ Sweet cherries, pears, plums and apples require cross-pollination to produce a crop of fruit. To ensure this, you need to plant at least two varieties of each fruit.

Throw them a bone

❀ When planting fruit trees, put in a few bones at the bottom of the planting hole. These will act as a slow-release fertilizer.

Feed the roots, not the trunk

❀ To make sure fertilizer reaches the roots of fruit trees, spread it in a circular band around the tree under the farthest spread of the branches. This is where the feeder roots are located, not up near the trunk.

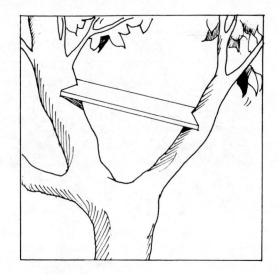

Let in more light

🦋 Open the center of your fruit trees to more sunlight and allow better penetration of insecticide and fungicide sprays. To do this, make a V-shaped notch in each end of a piece of lath of appropriate length, and wedge it between the trunk and limb of each of your fruit trees to widen the angle of the axil (the angle between the trunk and branch). Remove the lath in two years or so, when the limb has been trained to stay in place.

Spray them

🦋 Before spraying fruit trees that are near a vegetable garden, protect the vegetables by covering with a large sheet of plastic.

🦋 Spray the trees with dormant oil spray on a warm day (above 40° F.) in late winter before the trees' buds start to open. Dormant oil spray smothers many pests, but if applied too late in the season, it can damage the trees.

Prune them

🦋 Prune watersprouts from fruit trees in June.

Thin them

※ If the trees are overloaded with fruit, thin drastically to prevent the weight from breaking the limbs.

Support them

※ Even after thinning, the limbs may need support. Prop them up with boards. Tie a cloth to the limb, than nail the cloth to the board so wind won't make it fall from under the branch.

Keep your fruit

※ If the birds harvest more of your cherries and raspberries than you do, try planting the yellow varieties. Although they may still eat some of them, it seems the birds think the fruit is not ripe and won't eat as many as usual.

※ Try scaring the birds from your fruit trees with fake snakes. Cut an old garden hose into pieces about four feet long. Drape the pieces among the branches of the fruit trees.

※ Don't make the mistake of using bird netting to try to keep the birds from stealing your cherries. They get inside the netting from beneath, can't find their way back out, and so spend their time gorging on cherries.

※ If you are willing to go to a bit of trouble to save your strawberries from birds, slip the clusters of green berries into glass jars lying on their sides. Have the opening lower than the bottom end, in case of rain.

※ Keep birds from eating your grapes by slipping each bunch of grapes into a plastic bag to ripen.

Wash away frost

※ If a late frost catches your blooming fruit trees or strawberries, get out early (just before dawn), and rinse off the frost with the garden hose. It may not save all the blossoms, but will save enough to be worth the effort.

29

APPLES

Keep a clean orchard

❅ If your apples are lumpy, they probably have apple maggots. Fruit trees should be sprayed regularly, but another method of controlling pests for the coming year is to pick up and destroy all fallen fruit. Worms hide in the fallen apples and then pupate in the soil.

Wait till they are ripe

❅ Apples are ready to pick when they separate easily from the spurs. Hold an apple up; give it a twist. If it resists, let it ripen a few more days.

Best-ever applesauce

❅ Core apples but leave the peel on when making applesauce. Purée in the blender. Not only will you get more applesauce, but it will be more colorful and more nutritious.

BLACKBERRIES

Make picking easier

❅ For easier picking next summer, pinch out the growing tips of new blackberry canes when the canes are about hip-high. The next year's fruit clusters should be at the top of the plant, and easy to reach.

BLUEBERRIES

❅ Plant blueberries early in fall. Remove blossoms the following spring for healthy plants that will produce for many years.

❅ Blueberries need acid soil. Fill the planting hole with soil taken from beneath pine trees, including some pine needles. If pine soil isn't available, mix peat in with the soil.

❅ To feed blueberries, use azalea fertilizer. Don't feed at planting time; wait till the plants are well established.

❅ To further assure soil acidity, mulch with a thick layer of sawdust or pine needles. The mulch does double duty and also keeps weeds away.

❀ Because blueberries turn blue before they are actually ripe enough to pick, test to see that the berries come off stems easily. If you have to pull them, they are not ready.

CHERRIES
Cut out disease

❀ Black knot is a fungus disease that attacks cherries and plums. The branches swell and burst, and then the swelled part turns black. Cut out the diseased branches and destroy them.

Pit them easily

❀ Use a paper clip to make a handy cherry pitter. Bend the clip and use the large end as a handle. Scoop out the cherry pits with the small end.

❀ Another handy tool to pit cherries is a plastic drinking straw. Poke the straw through the cherry from the stem end, pushing the pit out the other side.

If they float, throw them out

❀ Cover freshly picked cherries with cold water. If some of them float, throw them out, because the floating cherries will invariably be wormy.

GRAPES

❀ Don't plant grape vines near flower or vegetable gardens. The vines are such heavy feeders with a widespread root system that they will rob nearby plants of nutrients and moisture.

The best food for great grapes

❀ Toss a few bones in the bottom of the planting hole when planting grapes. The phosphorus and potassium is good for them.

❀ Feed grape vines with phosphate and potash, not nitrogen. Nitrogen encourages lush green growth at the expense of fruit.

❀ Wood ashes spread around the base of your grape vines in May will give you sweeter grapes at harvest time.

Prune at the right time

❀ Prune grape vines while they are dormant, in late fall or very early in spring, so that they won't bleed excessively.

MELONS

❀ (See chapter 2, "Vegetables.")

PEACHES
Prevent problems

❀ To prevent brown rot on peaches, pick the fruit as soon as it turns yellow and let it ripen off the tree. Later, remove any mummies (shriveled fruit) from the tree; clean up fallen fruit and destroy it, as the disease can survive the winter inside it to infest next year's crop.

❀ In late spring and through the summer, cultivate frequently under peach trees to help get rid of peach borer and plum curculio. The insects pupate underground in cocoons about an inch below the surface.

❀ If your peach trees have peach borers, you can kill them with moth crystals (paradichlorobenzene). Spread the crystals in a circle around the tree, one and one-half inches away from the trunk. Mound soil over the crystals and up the trunk six to eight inches to cover the burrows made by the pests. The fumes enter the burrows and kill the borers. Remove the mound in about six weeks.

PEARS
Pick them early

❀ Pears are ready to pick if they come loose easily when you bend the stems horizontally.

🌺 Pick pears while they are firm for the best quality. Wrap each in newspaper and place in a shallow box or tray to ripen at room temperature. Do not have them touching each other. They should be ready to use in about a week.

Core them easily

🌺 Use the kitchen gadget meant for making melon balls to remove the cores from pears. Simply cut the pears in half and scoop out core and seeds with the melon-baller.

RASPBERRIES

Prune in late summer

🌺 After harvesting the berries, cut off the oldest raspberry and blackberry canes to ground level to encourage growth of new fruit-producing canes. Leave only six or seven new shoots per plant.

STRAWBERRIES

Plant at the right level

🌺 Strawberries must be planted with their crowns at soil level. Planted deeper, they rot; shallower, they dry out.

Keep them in rows

🌺 As you plant strawberries, lay strips of black plastic between the rows. If you don't do this, their vigorous runners will help them to spread quickly and fill in between the rows, making picking difficult. As runners form, guide them back to the row. The plastic helps in several ways: it prevents the strawberries from forming a thick patch, it smothers weeds, it conserves moisture, and it keeps the fruit from touching the soil, which can cause rot.

Don't let new plants fruit

🌺 Pinch off blooms of strawberry plants the first year they are planted for stronger, healthier plants with more fruit in the following years.

Well-fed strawberries

❀ Strawberries should be fertilized with a complete fertilizer such as 10-10-10. Fertilize after the plants are through bearing.

Save your strawberry plants, kill the aphids

❀ If your strawberries have aphids, make sure you destroy them for the next year by burning the patch. In early spring, spread a little straw over the plants and set it afire. The straw and dried leaves will burn, destroying aphids and eggs. The plants will not be harmed.

New beds for old

❀ Revitalize old strawberry beds by plowing under a strip one-third the bed's width on one side. Allow the runners to spread on the opposite side. Repeat the process the following two years, and you will have a completely new strawberry bed.

A new-fangled strawberry barrel

❀ An old-fashioned strawberry barrel is still a good idea. It lets you grow a lot of strawberries in a very small space. If you can't obtain a barrel, a dark green plastic garbage can will substitute nicely. Cut one-inch circular holes in staggered rows around the can. Put four inches of gravel in the bottom for drainage. Stand a piece of perforated plastic pipe, the same height as the can, in the center and fill it with gravel. This is to ensure that the water goes all the way to the bottom when you water your berries. Now fill with good soil up to the level of the lower holes, and plant them with strawberries. Fill up to the next row of holes; plant. Continue until the can is full, then plant six plants on top of the soil. Water well.

4
Storing the Harvest

Canning saves money

❀ If you have a vegetable garden that produces more than you can eat during the growing season, a pressure canner would be a wise investment. Although initially expensive, it will more than pay for itself within a few years. Pressure canning kills the organisms that cause food spoilage and is much safer than canning by the old-fashioned boiling-water-bath or open-kettle method.

Go to the experts

❀ Write to one of the companies that makes canning supplies for a book of instructions. Or write the Consumer Information Center in Pueblo, Colorado, or the United States Department of Agriculture, both of which also offer expert advice on canning all manner of fruits and vegetables.

Storing the canned produce

❧ Do not store home-canned goods in a damp basement or root cellar. The lids will rust, come loose, and the food will spoil.

❧ When storing home-canned goods, always put the newly prepared jars to the rear of the shelves, so the older jars get used first.

Freezing is easy

❧ Many vegetables and fruits may be frozen without blanching in boiling water. Just wash, box, and freeze. Try a sample of each kind and see how you like it.

Free freezer boxes

❧ Cottage cheese boxes make good freezer containers. Their only bad point is that, being round, they do waste some freezer space.

Keep small bags together

❧ When freezing in small bags such as sandwich bags, slip as many as possible into a plastic bread sack and close tightly. The second layer of plastic gives extra protection from freezer burn, and sacking them keeps them together and easier to find in the freezer.

No more hide and seek

❧ Be sure to label containers before you place them in the freezer. Remember to date the labels, so you can use the older food first.

Make a miniature root cellar

❧ Use a garbage can to make a miniature version of Grandma's root cellar. Bury the can, leaving the rim about six inches above the soil level to prevent water from getting inside. Store your apples, carrots or whatever in layers, with clean straw between each layer. Put the lid on the can and cover with a thick layer of straw or leaves to prevent freezing. Lay a few bricks or other weights on the straw so it won't blow away.

Storing in the cellar

❀ Don't set vegetables to be stored in a cellar directly on a concrete floor. Concrete draws moisture and may cause mildew.

❀ Check often to see if any of your stored produce is spoiling. Remove any that have bad spots.

APPLES

❀ Do not wash apples (or pears) before storing them. Moisture will encourage rotting.

CABBAGE
In the freezer

❀ If you find yourself overwhelmed by too many cabbages ready at once, try making this tasty freezer slaw. It is a good way to store extra cabbage, and is handy for winter meals. Grate one large cabbage; add one teaspoon of salt. Let stand one hour. Drain and squeeze the water out. Add one grated carrot and a grated ripe bell pepper. Now boil one cup of vinegar, two cups of sugar, one teaspoon of celery seed, and one teaspoon of mustard seed. Let cool, then pour over the cabbage mixture. Put into containers and freeze.

In the cellar

❀ To store cabbages, wrap each in several layers of newspaper and store at 33°–40° F.

❀ Cabbage can be stored for the winter in a cool frostfree place such as the cellar. Pull up the whole plant and hang upside down by the root. The outer leaves help prevent the head from shriveling, so leave them in place.

CARROTS
Leave them in the garden

❀ When fall and winter arrive, carrots can be left in the ground and harvested as needed. Before the severe weather, put a thick layer of mulch over the row. The mulch should keep the soil from freezing, and the carrots will stay fresh and crisp, better than if stored in the refrigerator.

MELONS
Soak them

❀ Submerge muskmelons for thirty seconds in water at 135° F. This inhibits mold and prolongs their storage life.

OKRA
Dry it

❀ Okra pods can be sliced crosswise and strung to dry for storage. When ready to use, soak the slices in water, then use the same water to cook them.

ONIONS
Sock them away

❀ Use old panty-hose for storing onions. Drop an onion into the toe and tie the hose in a knot above the onion. Add another onion, then another knot. Continue until the hose are filled. Hang in a cool dry place to store. When you need an onion, cut at the toe end, below the first knot.

Freeze them

❀ If stored onions begin to sprout, save them by chopping and freezing them. Freeze small amounts in a sandwich bag. It will be handy to grab a bag and dump it into your chili or whatever dish you are cooking.

PEAS
Freeze them quickly

❀ Cook or freeze peas as soon as possible after picking since, as with sweet corn, the sugar in peas quickly changes to starch.

PEANUTS
Dry them

❧ Peanuts should be allowed to dry before storing. Dry where mice can't get to them, then pick them from the plants and store in an airtight container. For a fresher taste, roast them as you use them, rather than all at once.

PEACHES
Keep them pretty

❧ Cover peeled sliced peaches with diluted orange juice (add four times the amount of water called for on the concentrate can) before freezing them. The orange juice keeps them from turning brown and adds a subtle but appealing flavor.

❧ Or, dip fruit in a solution of three tablespoons of lemon juice to one-half gallon of cold water before packing in boxes.

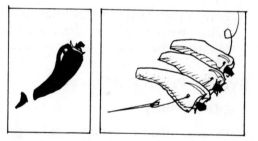

PEPPERS
Super-easy dried peppers

❧ Snip off the pointed ends of hot peppers to dry them for storage. This allows air to enter so they will dry more quickly. Use a large needle to string them like beads. Hang the string in your kitchen for handy access and as an attractive kitchen decoration.

POPCORN
Freeze it for maximum popping

❧ Your home-grown popcorn will pop better if you store it in an airtight container in the freezer. This also keeps bugs out of it.

POTATOES
Let them dry

❧ For less spoilage, let freshly dug potatoes air-dry in a frost-free place for a few days before storing in a cool dark place.

Keep them from sprouting

❧ Add a few apples to your stored potatoes. The apples give off ethylene gas, which helps to keep the potatoes from sprouting.

SQUASH
Don't pick too soon

❧ Winter squash keep best if left on the vines till mature. The rind will be hard when they are mature.

Leave on some stem

❧ Leave a four- to five-inch stem on each squash when you pick it, to make it keep better. Breaking off the stem can cause rot to start at the wound. Store in a cool frostfree place.

SWEET POTATOES
Dig them early

❧ Be sure to dig sweet potatoes before frost. Dig when the vines start to die. Let them air-dry in a warm place for a few days, then store at about 55° F.

TOMATOES
Have ripe tomatoes after frost

❧ Pick all your green tomatoes before the first killing frost in the fall. Wash them in a solution of two tablespoons of household bleach to one gallon of water. This bath helps prevent spoilage. Store at room temperature, placing the tomatoes so they don't touch each other. The green tomatoes will ripen and you can enjoy fresh tomatoes for weeks after the garden has stopped producing.

❧ If you want to ripen some of your green tomatoes in a hurry, put a very ripe apple with them. The apple gives off ethylene gas, which hastens ripening.

Freeze them easily

❧ Probably the easiest way to preserve tomatoes for winter is to freeze them. It is really simple to do. Select the most perfect fruits. Cut out the stems and any blemishes. Set them in a shallow pan and place in the freezer. When they are frozen solid, put them in large plastic bags, and back into the freezer. They will be separate, and you can take out as many or as few as you want at once. These are great in cooked dishes, but are too limp and mushy when thawed to be good in salads. Before using, hold them under hot water for a few seconds. The skin practically jumps off.

Make easy juice

❧ Don't waste time and effort making juice the old-fashioned way: scalding, peeling, cooking and running through a colander. Whew, what a job! Instead, just wash and core the tomatoes, cut away any bad spots, and run them through the blender, peel and all. Then can or freeze the juice. It is not only easier, but you keep more of the vitamins, too, since you are using the peels.

TURNIPS
Store away from other vegetables

❧ To prevent turnip odor from affecting other vegetables, store them on their own.

5

Herbs

Prepare the soil

- Most herbs need alkaline soil. Since most gardens have acid soil, sprinkle the herb bed with lime each spring.

- Herbs also need a soil with good drainage. A generous amount of compost and perlite or sand dug into the soil at planting time helps, and a raised bed is ideal.

Where to plant herbs

- Plant herbs in the sunniest spot available. Although most will survive in light shade, they will be healthier, more compact, and have a stronger flavor if grown in the sun.

- Plant your herbs as close to the kitchen as possible, so it will be handy to run out and snip what you need as you prepare your meals.

✀ Plant creeping herbs along a garden path. They will release a delightful fragrance when stepped on.

✀ Plant tall-growing herbs such as lovage and angelica at the back of the herb garden, shorter ones such as chives, thyme and parsley in front.

✀ Allow plenty of space for the spreading herbs such as rosemary, sweet marjoram and mint.

Plant seeds of annuals

✀ Most annual herbs can be easily grown from seeds. Sow the seeds in the garden, or get a head start by sowing them indoors. Transplant to the garden when the weather is settled.

✀ Soak parsley seeds to make them germinate more quickly. Soak overnight in warm water before planting. Parsley seeds not soaked before planting often take three weeks to germinate.

✀ Use a mixture of clean sand and sterile potting soil for starting herbs indoors from seed. Avoid potting soil that contains vermiculite, as it retains too much moisture and may cause the plants to rot, and can increase the likelihood of fungus attack.

✀ Skim milk makes a good substitute for fertilizer for herbs started indoors.

Buy plants of perennials

✀ Perennials (bay, rosemary, etc.) are sometimes difficult to start from seed. It is better to buy plants from a nursery.

Take cuttings from a friend's garden

✀ Many herbs root easily from cuttings. To take cuttings, use a clean sharp knife and cut off three to four inches of the stem tip, cutting at a node. Remove any flowers or buds, and the lowest set of leaves. Dip in a rooting hormone powder, shake off the excess, and stick in clean moist sand. Keep moist.

Some self-sow

❧ Many herbs self-sow: If the flowers are not removed, plants such as dill and sage produce seeds that fall around the parent plant and come up as "volunteers" the following spring.

When to plant

❧ Chives, sweet marjoram, thyme, sage, rosemary and bay should be started indoors from seed three months before the last spring frost date for your area.

❧ Basil, chervil and coriander seeds should be planted indoors two months before the last frost date.

❧ The following herbs can take some cold weather and may be planted early, about the same time you would plant lettuce: sage, chives, sweet marjoram, mint, oregano, parsley, tarragon and thyme.

❧ These herbs are more tender and shouldn't be planted outside till after your last frost date: bay, chervil, coriander, dill, rosemary and summer savory.

❧ Plant lavender seeds in the fall. The seedlings will appear in early spring.

Caring for herbs outside

❧ Most herbs need no fertilizer in the garden.

❧ They do not need much water, so water only during prolonged dry spells. They should not be mulched during the summer because the mulch keeps the soil too moist.

❧ If fungus develops on your herbs during wet weather, cut them back to encourage healthy new growth.

❧ Chemical insecticides should not be used on herbs, since you will be eating the plants. If you have a problem with pests, try this homemade remedy: Put some hot peppers and a few garlic cloves in the blender. Cover with water and blend thoroughly. Strain the mixture. Add one quart of water to the strained liquid and spray on the herbs. Don't get this hot mixture on your face.

❊ Perennial herbs may not survive a harsh winter without protection. When the soil freezes in early winter, mulch with a thick layer of straw, peanut hulls or other organic matter. Remove in early spring.

Harvesting herbs

❊ Keep snipping and using the tender tips of most herbs to encourage new growth.

❊ Most herbs have the most flavor and fragrance when harvested just before the flowers start to open.

Preserving herbs

❊ Many herbs are easily air-dried. Tie the stems in small bunches and hang upside-down in a warm, dark, dry place such as an attic. Dry until the leaves are crisp, then store in tightly closed jars.

❊ To get the most flavor from dried herbs, dry and store them with their leaves whole. Crumble the leaves when you are ready to use them.

❊ A good way to preserve herbs is to freeze them in water. Chop the herbs into an ice-cube tray and cover them with water. Freeze, and then store the cubes in plastic bags in the freezer. The cubes are very handy to add as you prepare soup or other dishes.

❊ Herbs may also be frozen whole. Place in plastic bags, seal and freeze. Chop when ready to use.

❊ To dry herbs in the oven, lay the stems on heavy paper on the oven shelf. Set the oven at 150° F. and leave the door open a few inches. Dry until the leaves are crisp. This may take several hours.

❀ Herbs can be quickly dried in a microwave oven. Place between two paper towels and dry for one minute. Remove from the oven, let cool, then test to see if the leaves are crisp. If not, return them to the oven for a few more seconds. Store in jars when crisp. Keep the jars in a dark place so they will keep their color.

❀ To save seeds from herbs such as dill and coriander, cut the mature flower stalks, and invert in paper bags to catch the seeds as they fall from the drying heads.

❀ In most cases, dried herbs are stronger-flavored than fresh, so use less in your recipes.

Growing herbs indoors

❀ For fresh herbs year round, grow them indoors in pots during the winter. Pot some up from the herb garden in the fall, before the first frost, or plant seeds in August. Grow in a sunny window to snip and use as needed. Chives, oregano, parsley, thyme, tarragon, basil and sweet marjoram all do well in pots.

❀ Most herbs planted in the garden will do well in poor soil, but when grown in containers the same herbs need a rich soil to thrive.

❀ To move a clump of chives indoors for winter use, pot some up in the fall, then sink the pot in the ground to its rim. Leave it outside for about two months of dormancy. Then trim the chives down to about three inches and bring inside to a sunny window.

❀ Treat mint the same as chives when bringing plants inside.

❀ To give potted chives a rest, cut them down to one inch above soil level, and place the pot in the refrigerator for two weeks. Then return the pot to a sunny window and watch the new burst of growth.

❀ If potted herbs turn brown on the leaf tips, it may be due to overcrowded roots. Repot in a pot one or two sizes larger.

Potpourri and arrangements

- Coriander seeds are a fragrant addition to potpourri.

- Granulated orris root should be added to potpourri to fix the fragrance. Keep in a tightly closed glass jar and shake it a few times each day for a week or two, until the fragrance is set.

- Use dried stems of herbs to make fragrant wreaths and dried flower arrangements.

ANGELICA

- Angelica dies if allowed to go to seed. Cut out flower stems before flowers go to seed.

BASIL

- Basil cuttings root easily in water.

- Keep basil leaves growing by pinching out the flowers as soon as they appear.

- Add basil, oregano and sweet marjoram to spaghetti sauce.

BAY

- In California bay and rosemary are outdoor perennials. If you live in a cold-weather area, grow them in containers so they can easily be moved inside for the winter.

CATNIP

- Grow some catnip for your cat's pleasure. Dry the leaves to use as stuffing for catnip toys. Cats also like to eat the fresh leaves.

- Catnip is a hardy plant, but since it spreads rapidly, it should be grown in a large pot or tub to contain its invasive habit.

- A pot of catnip in the house will help keep your cat out of your houseplants. He will eat the catnip leaves instead of nibbling your houseplants.

CHERVIL

- Chervil matures in six weeks, so if you want enough to harvest all summer, you must make successive plantings.

- Unlike most herbs, chervil does best when planted in light shade.

- Cut chervil leaves from the outside of the plant. New leaves will continue to grow from the center.

CHIVES

- Chives have a mild onion flavor. Use chopped raw chives to add flavor and color to soups, salads, fish and vegetable dishes.

- For winter use, chives are better frozen than dried.

- This herb can become a nuisance if allowed to go to seed and self-sow. Remove chive flowers before the seeds form.

- Flower stalks of chives are woody, so do not use them as flavoring for foods. Instead, dry them and use the lavender flowers in arrangements.

COMFREY

- Comfrey is rich in nitrogen, so any extra you have makes a great addition to the compost pile.

CRESS

- Sprout some cress seeds and use the hot sprouts as a spice. Sprinkle the seeds on a moist paper towel and cover with another towel. Roll up the towels and place in a plastic bag. Close the bag with a twist-tie and keep it in a warm spot for a few days. The sprouts will be very hot.

DILL

- You can use dill leaves and stems as well as the seeds to flavor pickles. Add two pieces of stem, with leaves, the height of the canning jar, to each jar of pickles you make.

❀ For a tasty dip, mix one tablespoon of prepared horseradish, one-third cup of chopped fresh dill leaves and one pint of sour cream. It's good and easy.

LAVENDER

❀ The blossoms of lavender are more fragrant than the leaves but both may be used to make delightful-smelling sachets for closets or drawers.

❀ Most herbs should be harvested before the flowers open, but lavender is an exception. Cut the stems when about half of the flowers on the spikes are open. Tie in bundles and hang upside down to dry in a warm, dark, airy place.

❀ Cut the first flowers to encourage a second crop.

❀ Rub your hands with lavender leaves to remove strong odors such as onion or garlic.

LEEKS

❀ Blanch leeks for a more delicate flavor. When they are nearly mature, tie newspaper around them or slip a six-inch-diameter drain tile over them, if the clump is small enough.

MINT

❀ If you want to grow mint, beware! It is very invasive and can quickly get out of control. It's a pleasant plant, in its place, but to keep it in its place, plant it in containers rather than directly in the garden.

❀ Most mints add a delightful flavor note to fruit punches and fruit salads. (Don't use pennyroyal in this way because pennyroyal can be toxic in large quantities.)

❀ For a delicious high-protein salad, combine chopped spearmint, parsley, cucumber, green onions and tomatoes with soaked-and-drained bulgur wheat. Add both lemon juice and olive oil to taste.

❧ Mint, chopped cucumber, pressed garlic and plain yogurt are a refreshing and cooling accompaniment to Indian curries. This is also good as a dressing on sliced tomatoes.

❧ Mint may be harvested often because it is fast-growing. In fact, if you harvest frequently, growth will be more vigorous.

NASTURTIUMS

❧ Use nasturtium blossoms and leaves in salads to add color and a tangy taste.

PARSLEY

❧ Parsley turns black when air-dried. To preserve the green color, and also for better flavor, parsley should be dried in the oven or microwave.

❧ Parsley is rich in vitamins A and C, and iron. Use it raw in salads to benefit fully from its good taste and nutritional value.

PENNYROYAL

❧ Help rid your pet of fleas. Boil a cupful of pennyroyal leaves and add the resulting tea to the rinse water when you bathe your pet. The pennyroyal will kill fleas and help to prevent reinfestation.

❧ For insurance between baths, rub the animal's coat with a handful of leaves.

ROQUETTE

❧ Pinch out flower buds to keep roquette from becoming bitter and tough.

ROSEMARY

❧ Use a pine-scented rosemary plant in a pot as a miniature Christmas tree.

SAGE

❦ Plant sage to lure bees and hummingbirds to the garden. They are attracted by the blue flowers.

❦ For something different, dip fresh sage leaves in beaten egg, then flour and pan-fry till lightly browned.

❦ Make a delicious sage bread: Dissolve three packages of dry yeast in two cups of warm water. Stir in one egg, one teaspoon salt, one-half cup sugar and one-fourth cup soft shortening. Add two cups whole wheat flour and one-fourth cup chopped fresh sage leaves. Gradually add four and one-half to five cups white flour, till the dough is not sticky. Shape into rolls and let rise till doubled in size. Bake at 400° F. until browned. This bread has a mild sage flavor. For a stronger flavor, add more sage. You can use the same recipe with other herbs, substituting them for the sage.

SALAD BURNET

❦ Like borage, salad burnet adds a mild cucumber flavor to fresh salads.

SAVORY

❦ Snip the tips of summer savory and use fresh all summer. In fall, before the first frost, cut and dry the plant. It is an annual and will not survive cold winters.

❦ Use savory as a salt substitute in vegetable dishes.

❦ Put several sprigs of savory in a bottle of vinegar and let it sit for several days. Use as a salad dressing. This may also be done with other herbs.

SWEET MARJORAM

❦ Sweet marjoram cuttings root easily.

❦ Get two harvests from your sweet marjoram. Cut the stems two to three inches above soil level when the plant starts to bloom. New shoots will appear. Harvest the second time when the plant flowers again.

❋ Use the sage bread recipe, substituting sweet marjoram. Wonderful with spaghetti.

TARRAGON

❋ French tarragon is the tarragon to grow. Russian tarragon has a very poor flavor and is also very invasive. You must buy plants to get the French type, as it does not produce seeds.

❋ Tarragon is also known as Little Dragon because of its intense flavor. Used sparingly, it adds an interesting taste to chicken, vegetables, salads and sauces, but too much is overpowering.

❋ Tarragon multiplies rapidly. To keep the plants healthy, divide about every three years, in the spring.

6
Flowering Plants

Buying plants

❀ When you buy bedding plants, you will probably be tempted by the plants that are already blooming. Resist the temptation. These larger plants are probably rootbound and won't do as well as smaller plants will. A little patience now will pay off with more flowers and healthier plants later.

Use the right fertilizer

❀ Too much nitrogen encourages lush green growth, at the expense of flowers. If you want lots of bloom from your flowering plants, feed them with a low nitrogen fertilizer such as 5-10-10. The first number indicates the nitrogen content.

Water early

❧ Water outdoor plants early in the day so they can absorb the moisture before the hot sun dries the soil. Early watering also gives the foliage a chance to dry before night comes. Wet foliage at night makes plants more susceptible to fungus diseases.

Make a path

❧ If you have pine trees, use some of the pine straw to make a path through your flower garden. The straw looks nice and will keep weeds from growing in the path.

Get more flowers

❧ Remove spent blossoms to keep your flowering plants blooming more. Snip blossoms off with scissors, so you don't damage the plants. Removing faded flowers, called dead heading, keeps the plant from making seeds. Since a flowering plant's primary goal in life is to reproduce itself, or produce seeds, it will try, try again . . . which means more flowers.

Flowering Bulbs

Extra-early blooms

❧ Plant spring flowering bulbs in a sheltered spot such as the south side of a building for extra-early flowers. They will bloom as much as two weeks earlier than the same varieties planted in an unprotected spot.

How deep to plant

❧ As a general rule of (green) thumb, plant flower bulbs at a depth equal to three times the diameter of the bulb.

A field of color

❧ Plant spring flowering bulbs in single-color groups, rather than mixed-color ones, for a more striking flower display.

Handle with care

❀ When planting bulbs, loosen the soil and make a hole with a trowel or other tool. Don't mash the bulb into the soil, or you may damage the basal plate (bottom of the bulb), causing it to rot.

A king-size bed

❀ The easiest way to plant flowering bulbs is to prepare the soil in the bed, then remove the soil to the proper depth for the type of bulb you're planting. Place the bulbs in the bed, and replace the soil. This is much quicker than digging individual holes for each bulb.

Longer-lasting blooms

❀ Extend the blooming season of bulb flowers by planting some early-flowering kinds, some mid-season and some late-blooming varieties. You can have daffodils and tulips in flower for several weeks.

Keeping track of bulb beds

❀ Mark bulb plantings with plant labels so you won't accidentally dig into them while they are dormant. You may think you can remember without labels, but it is very easy to forget the exact location if you have many flowers.

Squirrel-proof your bulbs

❀ Lay chicken wire over a newly planted bulb bed to keep squirrels from digging up the bulbs. The plants will grow through the chicken wire, but the squirrels can't get to the bulbs.

Gophers and chipmunks, keep out

❀ Keep gophers or chipmunks from tunneling into your flower beds and destroying your bulbs. Plant the bulbs in cans. Cut both ends from large fruit-drink cans. Bury the cans to their rims. Fill about one-third full of soil. Place one bulb in each can and finish filling with soil. The can acts as a barrier to keep the hungry rodents away from the bulbs.

Bulb nutrition

❧ Feed bulb flowers when leaves first come through the ground. They need little or no nitrogen, but do need phosphate and potash.

❧ Daffodils need phosphorus. Use bonemeal for small plantings or superphosphate for large plantings. Feed in spring before blooms appear, and in fall before the soil freezes.

No more mulch

❧ Remove any mulch from beds as soon as growth appears. Struggling through a heavy mulch is more damaging to the flowers than is the cold.

Leave the leaves

❧ Even though you may think the foliage of bulb plants looks messy or ugly when they are through flowering, resist the temptation to mow it off. The leaves are the food factories of plants. They manufacture food and send it to the bulb for storage in preparation for next year's flowers. If the foliage is removed, the plant is weakened and probably will not bloom. To beautify the bulb bed, plant shallow-rooted annuals such as petunias among the foliage, taking care not to damage the bulbs.

Bulb flowers in arrangements

❧ When cutting tulips or other bulb flowers for arrangements, cut in the green portion of the stem. If cut in the white portion, near the bulb, the flower cannot take up water and will quickly die.

❧ Put a copper penny in the vase with cut tulips to keep them from popping wide open.

❧ Try spraying cut tulips with hair spray to keep them from blasting (opening too fully).

Plant bulbs indoors for winter blooms

❦ In late September, pot tulips, daffodils or hyacinths in a mix-ture of one part peat, one part soil and one part sand or per-lite. The necks, or pointed ends, of the bulbs should be up, and partially visible above the soil line. Water and let the ex-cess water drain. Place in the lower part of the refrigerator. Leave the pots in the refrigerator until you see roots coming through the drain holes—about three months for tulips, two months for daffodils and hyacinths. Remember to water them as needed during the cold treatment. When the roots are visi-ble, take the pots from the refrigerator and put in a cool dark spot such as a closet, for about a week, then move them to a sunny window. You will be rewarded with bright colorful flowers in late winter, when they are most appreciated.

❦ Grow paperwhite narcissus or yellow Soleil d'Or narcissus for fragrant winter blooms. Just pot in gravel, which is only to anchor the plants, and water them. Place in a cool dark closet for two weeks, then bring to a cool window. When the flow-ers are spent, pitch them, because the forced bulbs will not bloom well again.

GLADIOLUS
Well-fed glads mean bigger blooms

❦ When your gladioli are about eight inches tall, scratch a little high-phosphorus fertilizer into the soil. Phosphorus content of fertilizer is indicated by the middle number of the fertilizer analysis listed on the package. Your glads will reward you with bigger blooms.

Extend the bloom season

❦ To lengthen the blooming period of your glads, do not plant them all at once. Instead, make three successive plantings, two weeks apart.

Make them multiply

❦ Gladiolus corms will multiply if you plant them shallowly at about three inches. When you dig them in the fall, remove the cormels and dust with a fungicide before storing. Store in a cool, dry, frostfree place until spring. Once again, plant at three inches. The tiny corms will not flower this season, but will grow larger. Store in the same manner at the end of the growing season. The following spring, plant at six inches and enjoy the many flowers.

Store properly

❀ Dig gladiolus corms when the leaves turn yellow. Cut off the foliage and store in a cool dry place in onion bags or old panty-hose.

❀ When you dig gladiolus corms to store them in the fall, dust with malathion to prevent thrips on next summer's flowers.

Flowering Annuals and Perennials

CHRYSANTHEMUMS
Get more flowers

❀ Mums should be pinched at least twice in early summer to make them produce more flowers. Pinch out the tips when they are six inches tall, then pinch again when they have grown another three inches.

Help them survive the winter

❀ If your outdoor mums don't survive the winter, the problem is probably too much moisture, rather than the cold temperatures. In late fall when the blooms have faded, dig the plants. Set them, with as much soil still attached as possible, on top of the ground in a protected place. Cover with a light mulch. In the spring, divide and replant them.

DAHLIAS

Grow them from seed

- Unwin hybrid dahlias may be grown from seed. They flower the first year and form tubers that can be dug in the fall and replanted the following spring.

Dahlias need warmth

- Wait until night temperatures are at least 50° F. before planting tender bulbs or tubers such as dahlias.

Cool storage

- To get dahlias ready for winter storage, cut the tops off after the first killing frost. The next sunny day that is above freezing, dig the tubers and turn the clumps upside down to dry for a few hours. Store in a cool, frostfree place, with some of the soil still clinging to the roots. The soil will help prevent the tubers from shriveling. The following spring, use a sharp knife to divide the clumps. Make sure each section you cut has a piece of the old crown attached, for this is where new growth will emerge.

DAYLILIES

Daylilies are good to eat

- The blossoms of daylilies are good to eat. Rinse the flowers, dry on paper towels, then dip in a thin pancake batter and pan-fry till lightly browned. They taste similar to fried mushrooms. *Don't pick the wild ones along highways, because they may have been sprayed.*

- Daylilies (and hibiscus) close at night, but you can keep them open for an evening party arrangement if you pick them as soon as they are open and place them in a plastic bag in the refrigerator. The longer the cold treatment, the longer they stay open. Prepare the arrangement ahead of time, but add the flowers at the last minute.

IRIS

More space to grow

✼ Crowded iris are susceptible to disease. Thin them to keep them healthy. To ensure bloom the following year, leave about one-third of the clump undisturbed. Dig up the rest, separate and lay in the sun to help seal the wound. Replant the next day. The following year, thin the section that was not disturbed.

LILY OF THE VALLEY

Too close for blooming

✼ Lilies of the valley quickly grow into a dense clump. If yours no longer bloom, they are probably too crowded, and need thinning.

✼ To keep lilies of the valley from drooping when you cut them for arrangements, try this trick that florists use. Mix one quart of cold water with one-fourth cup of Elmer's Glue. Submerge the flowers in the mixture for about ten minutes. Let the flowers dry, then make your arrangement. They will hold up their heads beautifully.

NASTURTIUM

Nasturtiums prefer neglect

✼ These easy-to-grow annuals do well when planted in poor soil and prefer rather dry conditions. Choose a sunny spot, plant when danger of frost is past and watch these favorites thrive.

Color your garden beautiful

✼ Nasturtiums have a long flowering season—one month from sowing until frost—and come in such a wide variety of colors that they are a wonderful addition to any flower garden. Hybrid colors range from palest cream through bright yellow and oranges to dark reds and mahogany.

PEONIES

Superblooms

✿ Remove tiny side buds from peonies as soon as they form. The main flower will grown larger and more beautiful since it doesn't have to share the nutrients.

✿ If you have a fireplace or woodstove, scatter some of the wood ashes around your peonies. They will benefit from the potash content of the ashes.

Divide and conquer

✿ When peonies are transplanted, the shock often prevents them from blooming for at least two years. To divide them and still have flowers the following season, dig up only half of the clump and transplant. The following year, transplant the other half.

PETUNIAS

For portable color

✿ Plant petunias (or mums) in large pots for portable color. Grow them in a sunny spot, then move them to the patio or porch for temporary decoration. They can stand a few shady days at a time, but move them back into the sunshine to keep them bright and blooming.

For winter color

✿ If you want to bring some of the summer's petunias inside for winter bloom, cut them back to about four inches to force new growth. Spray with insecticide before bringing them in, to avoid carrying white flies and other pests in with the plants.

POPPIES

When to plant

✿ Plant Oriental poppies in September. Mulch in winter with a three-inch layer of leaves or straw, if you are in a cold-weather area.

How to get more

❀ Oriental poppies may be propagated in late summer by root cuttings. Dig up a plant and cut the roots into six-inch sections. Plant the sections three inches deep. When the ground freezes, protect with a heavy mulch. Remove the mulch in early spring.

Don't let them go to seed

❀ Volunteer poppy seedlings (produced from self-sowing) are inferior, so remove the seed pods to prevent self-sowing.

❀ To use Oriental poppies, poinsettias and other bleeders as cut flowers, cut them early in the day as they open. Immediately sear the stem end by holding it in a flame for a few seconds. This seals the stem so it won't bleed, but it can still take up water.

ROSES
Plant them right

❀ To grow strong healthy rose bushes, plant them correctly. Plant them where they will receive several hours of sun each day. Soak bare-root plants in a bucket of warm water overnight before planting. Remove the pot from container-grown plants; also remove any twine or wires that may be on the plant. Dig a hole large enough that the roots won't be crowded. Make a mound of soil in the hole and spread the roots over the mound. Fill the hole half-full of good soil, water well. When the water has soaked into the soil, finish filling the hole. The bud union should be just above the soil level.

❀ When planting roses, mound a hill of soil about eight inches high around the stems to prevent them from drying out. When new growth appears, this is a sign that the roots have become established, and you can safely remove the extra soil.

Get more flowers

❀ Enjoy your roses doubly. Cut lots of flowers for arrangements, and cut those flowers left on the bush when they fade.

Cutting induces branching and formation of more buds. Cut just above the second leaf with five leaflets unless new sprouts have already started above that location.

Get more bushes

- Try air-layering your favorite rose bush to get more like it. Use a sharp knife and cut three-fourths of the way through the cane, cutting just below a node. Insert a toothpick in the cut to keep it open. Wrap the wound with damp sphagnum moss and pack some of the moss into the cut. Seal the moisture in by wrapping tightly with plastic wrap. Close the plastic wrap by taping at the top and bottom with plastic tape. When you see roots growing through the moss in a few weeks, cut the new plant from the mother bush and plant it. The new plant may not be as hardy as the original, since most roses are grafted onto a hardy rootstock. Be sure to protect it in winter.

Feeding roses

- Feed once a month, starting as soon as leaf buds begin to pop open.

- Do not fertilize roses after August. It will encourage tender new growth that will be winter-killed if you are in a cold-weather area.

Roses as cut flowers

- Take a jar of water with you when cutting roses. Place the stems in the water immediately after cutting. When you bring them inside, hold the stems under water and recut, cutting on a slant. Cutting underwater prevents air from entering their water conducting tubes and prolongs their lives.

- For long-lasting cut roses, cut them in the evening. The plant has manufactured and stored food in the stem during the day. Bring the cut roses inside immediately and place the stems in hot water, as hot as you would use for washing dishes. Add Floralife or another rose preserver and let the roses stand until the water cools before making your arrangement.

❀ Make several shallow cuts in the portion of the stem that will be underwater in the vase. Water will enter through the cuts. Make sure there are no cuts above the water level, for then they will prevent the water from going up to the flower head.

SUNFLOWERS
They like it wet

❀ Sunflowers are thirsty plants, so use them in the garden to help dry up wet spots.

Save the seeds

❀ If you want to harvest your sunflower seeds, cover the flower heads with nylon net and tie down ends with string. This keeps the seed from falling off and keeps the birds from making off with them.

Flowering Vines

The glory of morning glories

❀ A plain fence can be turned into a beauty spot if you plant flowering vines along its length. Morning glories and thunbergia (black-eyed Susan vine) are good choices for quick bloom. They need full sun. If the fence is solid, such as a wooden fence, tack up some heavy twine to support the vines.

Keeping honeysuckle under control

❀ Such beautiful flowering vines as honeysuckle, trumpet vine and passion flower are so invasive you have to make sure they have room to spread—or that you have the energy to fight to keep them within bounds!

A practical beauty

❀ Grow scarlet runner beans for double benefits. Enjoy the beauty of the bright red flowers, and eat the beans.

CLEMATIS
Sun and shade

❀ For a healthy clematis with lots of flowers, provide it with a sunny location with shade at its roots. Sound tricky? Just plant annual flowers at its base.

Support your local vines

❀ Clematises don't cling to trellises or supports; they must be tied. Use strips of panty-hose, which are strong yet won't damage the vine. If it's growing up a stone or concrete wall, press plastic wood in graduated steps up the wall and let it harden. Then drive staples or small nails into it. Tie twine to the nails.

Protective collars for clematis

❀ Injuries to the base of the clematis vine can be fatal. Protect it from mower injury by growing it in a collar. Make the collar from an eight-inch clay flower pot. Carefully break out the bottom, starting at the drain hole and chipping it away. Slip it over the new plant. Plants already too large for slipping the collar over may be protected by placing bricks or stones around them to keep the mower away.

Secrets of sound pruning

❧ Some types of clematis bloom on the current year's growth and should be pruned in late winter. *C. x jackmanii* and *C. lanuginosa* are in this group. Other types bloom on last year's growth and should be pruned after flowering. *C. montana* and *C. florida* are in this group.

WISTERIA

❧ The best time to prune wisteria is before it leafs out, so prune in late winter.

Cut Flowers

Make them last

❧ Cut flowers will have days of extra life if handled properly. Cut them either early in the day or in the evening, using a sharp knife and cutting at a slant. Strip off any foliage that will be underwater in the vase. Rotting foliage builds up bacteria and quickly kills the flowers. Submerge the flowers in warm water at about 100° F. for one-half hour. Put them in a clean vase and let them air-dry. Change the water every day and recut the stems every three days.

❧ Cut flowers when they are only half-open to enjoy your arrangements much longer.

❧ Don't set fresh flower arrangements on the TV. The heat from the television will quickly make the flowers die.

❧ Keep arrangements in a cool room away from hot- or cold-air vents. Also keep them out of direct sun.

❀ Flower preservative should always be added to the water for a cut flower arrangement. It will add several days' life to the flowers. Either buy preservative from a florist or else mix one tablespoon of white Karo and one teaspoon of Clorox to a quart of water. The Karo feeds the flowers, while the Clorox kills rot-producing bacteria.

❀ Everyone puts corsages in the refrigerator to make them last longer. If there is fruit in the refrigerator, this will actually shorten their life. Fruit gives off ethylene gas which makes flowers go to sleep. If you want to refrigerate your corsage along with fruit, seal it in a plastic bag so the gas can't get to it.

Here's a handy frog

❀ Turn a plastic-mesh strawberry basket upside-down and anchor with florist's clay in a bowl or vase to use as a frog for flower arranging.

Clean vases easily

❀ Soak glass or crystal vases in vinegar or strong tea to remove lime deposits.

MAKE SOME PERMANENT ARRANGEMENTS

How to preserve flowers

❀ Many flowers will dry beautifully for winter bouquets if you tie them in bunches by their stems and hang them upside down in a warm, dry, dark place such as the attic. Celosia (cock's comb), gomphrena (globe amaranth) and bells of Ireland are just a few that can be easily dried. Pick as soon as the flowers open and dry till they are crisp. Then spray with hair spray to help preserve them.

❀ Dry flowers with a mixture of two parts borax and one part white cornmeal. Pick the flowers with about one inch of stem attached. Bury the blossoms in the mixture, in a box that can be sealed. Whether the flowers should be placed face up or down depends upon the type of flowers they are. Flat flowers like daisies should be face down; roses, zinnias, etc., should be face up. Use a spoon to pour the drying mix into crevices between the petals. Dry several flowers at the same time, but be sure they are not touching. Seal the box. Check every day to see if they are ready. Drying time varies according to the type of flower. When they are dry, add a wire stem to each flower, tape with florist's tape, and make your arrangement. The drying mix can be used many times. When it becomes moist, bake at 200° F. for about an hour.

❧ Use glycerine to make flowers and foliage permanent for winter bouquets. Use a solution of one cup of glycerine to one quart of hot water. Submerge the plants for several hours or merely place their stems in it. When you see drops of moisture forming around the edges of the leaves, they are ready. Remove from the solution and hang upside down to dry. They will be leathery, not brittle. Add one teaspoon of Clorox to the solution to kill bacteria. It can be reused many times. Glycerine can be bought at most drug stores.

Make a pressed-flower picture

❧ Press some small flowers such as daisies and violets between several layers of newspaper. Lay a heavy book on top. In about two weeks the flowers will be dried and ready to use for a dried-flower picture. Glue a piece of plain fabric to a piece of cardboard the size of your picture frame. Glue the flowers to the fabric in an attractive arrangement. Let dry, frame, and enjoy on your wall or sitting on a shelf or table.

Make your own planters

❧ Recycle an old tire and make a pretty planter. Use a strong sharp knife and cut off the bead on one side. Then cut the side of the tire in a zigzag pattern. Now turn the tire inside-out. Set the tire planter on an old wheel and paint both black. Fill the wheel with gravel, the tire with soil, and plant your flowers. This looks like an expensive flower urn, instead of an old tire.

❧ Use cement blocks to make a planter that is good for annuals, herbs or strawberries. Place four blocks, holes up, in a rectangle, two side by side, and one at each end. Lay another block on top, in the center. Fill the holes with soil and plant.

❀ Do you think cement planters are pretty but too heavy to be practical? You can make some that are fairly light in weight by using three parts vermiculite to one part cement. Add enough water to thoroughly moisten the mixture and trowel it into your form. An easy way to make a bowl-shaped form is to make a depression in a pile of sand.

❀ Use a child's wagon for a planter for annual flowers. Make a few holes in the bottom for drainage, fill with soil and plant. It is so handy when it is time to mow the lawn—there's nothing to mow around; just pull the flower wagon to an area that is already mowed.

Preserve wood planters

❀ Wooden window boxes should be treated with copper naphthanate to prevent decay. It also kills disease organisms. Some of the other wood preservatives such as creosote are toxic to plants.

7

Lawns and Groundcovers

Planting a New Lawn

Prepare the lawn area

❀ Prepare the soil in summer for fall seeding. This gives weed seeds a chance to germinate and be eliminated before you plant the grass.

❀ Prepare the soil for a new lawn by tilling about eight inches deep. Remove stones and other debris. Rake to level, but with a slight slope away from the house to help prevent water from standing. Water the soil to settle it. When it is dry enough, rake again, fill in any low spots, and plant.

❀ Lawns should have a grade of about six inches per one hundred feet to allow excess water to run off.

❀ If your lawn is on a hill, and an extreme grade can't be avoided, there should be a retaining wall to form a terrace.

✻ Toadstools in the lawn may indicate poor drainage. Poor drainage contributes to diseases. Provide adequate drainage and fill in low spots. This is a job that needs to be done before you plant the lawn. In extremely wet areas, you may need to put in drainage ditches.

Choose the right grass

✻ Ask your nurseryman for the best type of grass seed for your area. Consider the amount of sun or shade your lawn will receive.

✻ Cheap grass seed often contains weed seeds; buy good quality seed.

✻ A mixture of several varieties will make a more successful planting than just one or two varieties.

✻ If you have trouble growing a nice lawn, plant zoysia. Zoysia is a tough grass, long-lived and easy to care for. It grows slowly and doesn't require mowing as often as other grasses. It is disease- and pest-resistant. However, it does turn brown for a longer period in winter.

Sow seeds in fall

✻ Fall is the best time to sow grass seed. Grass sown in spring is often killed by hot, dry summer weather.

✻ Fall sowing helps keep crabgrass and other weeds from taking over, since the weeds grow more slowly in cool weather.

Plant correctly

✻ Use about four pounds of grass seed per thousand square feet of new lawn.

✻ Broadcast grass seed for the new lawn twice: first by walking north and south as you sow, then walk east and west and sow again. This gives better distribution of the seeds.

✻ Scratch up the soil with a rake; sow the seeds. Don't cover the seeds with soil; they need light to germinate. Keep the area moist until the young plants are growing well. When the grass is about two inches high, mow, cutting off about one-half inch the first cutting.

※ For more vigorous growth, spread a very thin mulch of clean straw over newly seeded areas. The straw shades delicate seedlings from the hot sun and helps preserve moisture in the soil, yet lets enough light through for germination.

※ Grass seed sown on a slope should be covered with burlap to keep it from washing away. Remove the burlap when the grass begins to grow.

Care for the new lawn

※ If there are bare spots in your new lawn, reseed immediately to keep weeds from getting started.

※ Mower wheels will damage a new lawn if you mow when the ground is wet.

Planting sod

※ Use sod rather than seed to plant steep slopes.

※ Roll a newly sodded area to make a smooth surface and to be sure the roots are in contact with the soil.

Planting plugs

※ Zoysia is planted by plugs rather than by seed. Plant the plugs about one foot apart each way. Water well. Keep weeds out by pulling until the zoysia spreads enough to choke them out.

Caring for the Established Lawn

Feed the lawn

※ Fertilize the lawn the first time in mid-February so the first growth gets the benefit. Fertilize again in early fall.

❀ Grass growing under shallow rooted trees such as maples will be robbed of nutrients and may need extra feeding.

❀ Water the lawn after spreading fertilizer to get the food to the roots where it is needed.

Water the lawn

❀ Deep watering once a week encourages deep root systems, resulting in hardy plants. Daily shallow watering promotes shallow roots, which can mean weaker plants which will suffer if you must be away and miss watering as usual.

❀ Shallow watering encourages crabgrass, which has shallow roots. It also uses more water and wastes more through evaporation.

❀ Apply at least one inch of water in cool parts of the country, two inches in hot areas, approximately once a week in dry weather. To tell how much you're watering, set a few cans around on the lawn and measure the amount of water they catch.

❀ To prevent wasteful drift run the sprinkler when there is no wind.

Mow the lawn

❀ Different types of grasses need to be mown at different heights. Zoysia and Bermuda bent grass should be cut to about three-fourths of an inch, while Kentucky bluegrass should only be cut to one and a half or two inches.

❀ Don't cut off more than two inches in height of grass at a cutting, lest the grass plants go into shock. It is better to mow more often, cutting off less than two inches at a time.

❀ To prevent thatch buildup, use a lawn sweeper to remove grass clippings. They are full of nitrogen, so add them to the compost pile or use as garden mulch.

❀ If thatch is not a problem, leave grass clippings on the lawn for self-fertilization. The clippings are rich in nitrogen.

73

Get rid of weeds

✿ Mid-February is the time to apply a preemergence herbicide to control crabgrass. It must be applied before the seeds start to germinate.

✿ Broadleaf weeds in the lawn can be killed by a selective herbicide. A few drops should be poured directly on each weed to prevent damage to ornamental plants.

✿ If you want to remove weeds by hand, you must get roots, crown and all. If you merely break off the above-ground part, new shoots will spring up.

✿ Take care when applying broadleaf weed killers to the lawn. They will also kill desirable garden plants. If you spray, never do it on a windy day.

Get rid of insects

✿ Circles of dead grass in the lawn in late summer are an indication of chinch bugs. Adults are tiny, about one-eighth to one-fourth inch long, with black and white patches on their backs. Apply an appropriate insecticide.

✿ Sod webworms do their worst in early summer. They feed at night and hide by day so it is hard to see them, but they are green worms about three-fourths of an inch long. The adult is a brown moth. Use Sevin or diazinon, or for biological control, dipel. Treatment may need to be repeated in two or three weeks.

Seed bare spots

✿ If your lawn has bare spots from winter kill, sprinkle grass seed on the spots in March. Don't dig it in, just sprinkle it on. Digging it in encourages weed and crabgrass seeds to germinate.

Make trimming easier

✿ Eliminate hand trimming by using brick or concrete edgings, flush with the soil, around flower beds, buildings, etc.

※ Walks should be flush with the lawn.

※ If you must trim around trees, etc., by hand, try using hedge pruning shears instead of grass cutters. The shears take a bigger bite and will get the job done more quickly.

※ If you use the string-type grass trimmers, be careful when trimming around young trees. The trimmers can girdle the trees, causing them to die.

Roll lumpy lawns

※ Early spring is the best time to roll the lawn.

※ Never roll a lawn when it is wet. It causes compaction.

Fall and winter care

※ Don't let fallen leaves remain on the lawn. Leaves should not be burned; they can be used to add humus to the garden. Buy snow fencing and make a leaf pen. Pile it full of leaves. Over the winter, they will settle and partially rot. In spring add a layer of them to the garden and till it in.

※ In late winter, remove any accumulation of leaves that may have blown up around fences or buildings. As the weather begins to warm up, these soggy leaves will not only smother the grass, but will also encourage disease.

※ When you rake leaves, you can speed the job by using an old sheet. Spread the sheet on the lawn; rake the leaves onto it. Take the sheet by all four corners and pull it to the leaf bin or compost pile. Dump the leaves and go back for another load.

※ Frozen grass is easily damaged, so for a pretty summer lawn, avoid walking on it in the winter.

Problem areas

※ Use black plastic to turn a problem area of your lawn into an oasis of beauty. If you have a place that can't be reached with the lawnmower, keep the weeds from growing by covering it

with black plastic. Add a thin layer of pea gravel to the laye
of plastic. Plant creeping sedum in the gravel. The sedum wi
grow well in the gravel, but weeds won't. Finish your min
garden by adding a birdbath, driftwood or an interestin
stone.

Groundcovers

Where to use them

❀ Groundcovers are good to use in shady spots where gras
won't grow. Along borders, on hillsides that are difficult t
mow, around stepping stones, around fish pools, any plac
where the lawnmower won't go are good places to us
groundcovers.

❀ Don't plant groundcovers where they will be walked on. Mos
can't take it.

Improve the soil

❀ While groundcovers are usually vigorous plants, befor
planting them you should improve the soil as you would d
for other plants. Dig it to a spade's depth, remove weeds, an
add compost or rotted manure.

Plant closely

❀ You will get quicker coverage and have less of a weed prob
lem if you get out small starts of groundcover plants fairl
close together, about six inches each way. As the plant
spread, they will smother weeds, but until they do, cultivat
or hand-pull the weeds.

Good groundcovers to use

❀ Violets and lily of the valley make excellent groundcovers
quickly spreading to fill in bare spots. Violets do well in su
and light shade; lily of the valley does well in both light an
heavy shade.

❀ There are many good groundcovers. Some evergreen ones for shade are: creeping myrtle or *Vinca minor*, pachysandra, English ivy or *Hedera helix*, wintergreen or *Gaultheria procumbens*, partridge berry or *Mitchella repens*.

❀ Some good deciduous groundcovers for shade are: hostas, sweet woodruff (*Asperula odorata*), *Phlox subulata*.

8
Trees
and Shrubs

Don't plant here

❦ Shrubs or perennials are often planted in one of the worst possible places: under the house overhang. They may look pretty there, but they are almost sure to suffer from insufficient moisture unless you are prepared to water often. The overhang keeps moisture from reaching the roots in all but the heaviest rainfall.

❦ Plan ahead when planting trees. Be sure to plant them far enough apart that they will have plenty of space when they are mature, and do not plant under power or telephone wires.

❦ Don't plant trees near tile systems, septic tanks, etc. If planted too close, the tree roots will clog the systems in their search for water, causing either costly removal, or if you do the job yourself, much hard work which is easier avoided in the first place.

❧ Don't plant trees within six feet of sidewalks or concrete fish pools, as the growing roots may crack the concrete.

Plant in spring or fall

❧ Trees, shrubs and evergreens should be planted in early spring so they will be well rooted and able to withstand the summer heat, or else early in the fall so they will be off to a good start before the harsh winter weather.

Plant them right

❧ When you dig the planting hole, make two piles of soil, with the topsoil in one and the soil from the bottom of the hole in the other. When the tree is in place, start filling in with the topsoil so it will be in contact with the tree's feeder roots. Put the less fertile soil on top.

❧ With the exception of dwarf fruit trees, most trees should be planted a couple of inches deeper than they were in the nursery. You should be able to see a mark on the trunk of each tree.

❧ In spite of common belief, it is not necessarily a good idea to mix peat or other soil additives with the soil in a planting hole for trees or shrubs. The roots like the improved soil, and so confine themselves to it, rather than spreading to the surrounding soil as they should.

❧ Always remove any wires or twine from young trees as you plant them. If left on the tree, the wire will girdle the tree as it grows, eventually killing it.

❧ Keeping trees at the proper level when planting can be difficult because the soil settles. Solve this problem by laying a narrow board across the planting hole and tying the tree to the board at the proper level. Leave this in place for a few days until the soil is settled.

❧ Before container-grown shrubs or trees are planted, some of the soil should be rinsed from their root balls so the root tips are exposed. Plant immediately. The exposed roots will penetrate the new soil. Without this treatment, many times the roots refuse to leave the original soil, and end up strangling the plant.

🌿 Make a shallow depression in the soil around newly planted trees or shrubs for a watering basin. The water will soak into the soil instead of running off.

🌿 Always brace young trees at planting time to be sure they will grow straight. Use a heavy wire, threaded through a piece of garden hose. Place the hose at one end of the wire and loop it around the tree. Stake the other end securely to the ground. Use three braces, placing them equidistantly around the tree.

Keep them watered

🌿 In fall and early winter, don't forget to water new trees and shrubs. Continue until the ground freezes.

Use a mulch

🌿 Mulch around newly planted trees to conserve moisture and smother weeds.

🌿 Mulch acid-lovers such as azaleas and rhododendrons with pine needles or oak leaves.

How and when to prune

🌿 Trees and shrubs that are being transplanted suffer from root loss. To minimize the shock, prune the branches back one-third of their length. This cuts down the rate of water loss through the leaves, putting less of a strain on the plant.

🌿 Prune spring-flowering shrubs just after flowers fade. Fall or spring pruning will mean no flowers.

🌿 Break the candles (new growth) of evergreens back to the halfway point to make the evergreens more compact and bushy. This is best done in early summer.

🌿 Prune away damaged or dead evergreen branches. They are an invitation to attack by diseases and insects, as well as a blight to the plant's appearance.

※ When pruning large limbs, always undercut first. This means to cut from the bottom up, one-third of the way through the limb, then finish by cutting from the top. The undercut keeps the limb from splitting and breaking off, which could damage the trunk and become an entryway for insects and diseases.

※ If your old flowering shrubs bloom poorly, you can induce better bloom by pruning. The first year, cut out one-third of the large and one-third of the medium trunks at ground level. Repeat in early spring two more years. After the third pruning, you will have a completely new bush.

※ Shrubs should always be pruned so that the lower portion will be wider than the top, so it can get plenty of sunlight. Properly pruned shrubs will retain their lower leaves for a fuller, more attractive appearance.

Don't use wound paint

※ It is usually better not to use tree-wound paints after pruning. They slow healing and sometimes even promote decay.

Wash off mites

※ Wash off spider mites from evergreens with a hard spray of water from the hose. Repeat several times at three-day intervals. Yellowing foliage on evergreens may be an indication of mites. Hold a sheet of white paper under a branch and shake the branch. If you see tiny moving specks on the paper, they are mites.

Protect trees and shrubs

※ Wrap chicken wire loosely around newly set trees to prevent damage from gnawing rabbits.

※ Put a chicken-wire cage around tender shrubs and loosely fill with straw for a good winter protection.

Prepare for moving

※ If you have a shrub or small tree you want to move, prepare it by root-pruning it first. Use a spade and cut around the sides of the soil ball you will be moving. Leave the tree in place for a few days to recover from the shock of root loss. Finish digging and replant.

Get more with cuttings and layering

❧ Try taking cuttings of evergreens in January to start your own tree nursery. Juniper, yew, cedar and arborvitae are some of the more easily rooted evergreens. Take five-inch cuttings, using a sharp knife. Dip the cut ends in rooting hormone powder. Stick the cuttings in moist coarse vermiculite or soilless mix. Keep in bright light in a cool place. Set out in a protected spot in spring. Transplant to permanent settings the following year.

❧ Shrubs and woody vines are often difficult to propagate, but with patience, they can be propagated by layering. It takes time, but is usually successful. Carefully bend a branch down and bury a section of it in the soil. It should be about three inches deep. Hold it in place with a hairpin-shaped wire, and place a stone or brick on top. It may take up to two years, but eventually roots will form and the new plant can be separated from the parent plant.

Plant a windbreak

❧ Plant two or more rows of evergreens such as pine, spruce or fir as a windbreak and you can save about 25 percent on winter fuel bills. Plant them closely spaced in the rows. They should be from 20 to 45 feet from the house, on the windward side.

Holly takes two

❧ If you want to grow holly with its pretty red berries, you must plant at least two shrubs. Hollies are either male or female, and only the female produces the berries, but a male is necessary for pollination. One male shrub is enough to pollinate five or six females. Ask your nurseryman to help choose, so you will get the right number of each sex.

9
Ferns

Recognize the spores

❧ Ferns' fertile fronds have spores (cases of reproductive cells) on their undersides in a regular pattern. Many people mistake these spore cases for insects. Ferns aren't often bothered by insects, but when they are, you will notice that pests do not form so neat a pattern as the spores do.

Collect the spores

❧ Break off a piece of frond which has ripe spores. Put it in a plastic bag. Leave the bag open so the frond can air-dry. The spores will fall out in the bag.

Plant the spores

❧ Fill a clean container with a sterile potting mix. Moisten the mix and sow the spores on top. Cover with glass or clear plastic. Put in a warm place out of direct sun. Keep moist. In about two months, you will see tiny green discs forming, followed by tiny ferns.

Indoor Ferns

General growing requirements

❧ Grow indoor ferns in a north or west window. Keep constantly moist, but not soggy. Fertilize once a month, except during winter, with soluble houseplant fertilizer.

Most indoor ferns need temperatures from 55° to 70° F., relatively high humidity, and indirect light. Keep out of drafts.

Use equal parts garden soil (sterilized in the oven at 200° F. for an hour), sand and compost for indoor ferns. Use commercial potting soil in place of compost if compost isn't available.

Make a fern ball

❧ Make a pretty hanging fern ball. Buy two wire baskets from a florist or garden center. Line with moist unmilled sphagnum moss and fill the center with the potting mix described above. Place a piece of cardboard on top of each basket and flip it over. Poke several ferns securely into the bottom and sides of each basket. Turn one basket upright. Place the other on top of the upright one. Gently slide the cardboard from between the baskets and wire the two baskets together to form a ball. Suspend with a wire in a shady, protected place outdoors in summer, or indoors. Keep moist.

ASPARAGUS FERN

❧ Asparagus ferns are easily grown from fresh seed. They are slow to germinate, so be patient. They are not a true fern, since true ferns produce spores, not seeds.

BOSTON FERN

❧ Boston ferns are among the easiest of the indoor ferns. Keep evenly moist in a brightly lit spot out of direct sun. They can have some sun in winter.

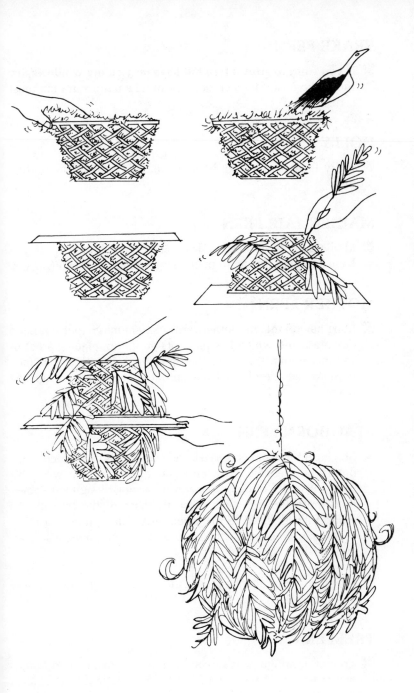

BRAKE FERN

❀ If you want to grow a fern but have only sunny windows, try the brake fern, *Pteris cretica*. It can take more sun than most ferns.

HOLLY FERN

❀ Holly ferns like a slightly acid soil. Add peat to the potting mix.

MAIDENHAIR FERN

❀ Maidenhair ferns need at least 50 percent humidity. If you have had poor luck with them, try growing one in a terrarium.

MOTHER FERN

❀ Start new plants of mother fern, *Asplenium viviparum*. Bend down a frond which has plantlets on its tip, placing a pot of soil mix under it. Anchor the tip to the soil with a U-shaped wire. When the plantlet has sprouted roots, cut it from the frond.

STAGHORN FERN

❀ Staghorn ferns are epiphytes and should not be planted in ordinary potting soil. Grow on a slab of osmunda or wood. To grow on wood, put a large handful of moist long-fiber sphagnum moss on the wood; place the base of the fern on the moss, then tie it all to the wood with fishing line. Water by soaking in a bucket or the sink. As the fern grows, it will attach itself to the wood.

❀ Staghorns may also be grown in pots. Use a mixture of bark and osmunda. Water often.

TREEFERN

❀ Treeferns are gorgeous exotic plants and make good houseplants because they don't need the high humidity that most ferns demand.

- Hawaiian treeferns, *Cibotium chamissoi*, are easily grown in water. Place a trunk section upright in a bowl of water so the lower third is submerged.

Outdoor Ferns

General growing requirements

- To have a healthy outdoor fern garden, add as much leaf mold as possible to the soil before planting. If leaf mold is not available, substitute peat.

- There is no need to fertilize outdoor ferns, but compost or leaf mold around the plants is helpful.

- Don't wet the fronds when watering ferns. Soak the soil by running water slowly from a hose placed at the base of the ferns.

- Rock ferns need a light sandy soil with some lime added.

- Try to reproduce the conditions of the fern's natural habitat in the garden. They need humus-rich soil, plenty of moisture, and shade. Planted in a dry, sunny place, they won't survive.

Some need lime

- Some ferns need alkaline soil. Add lime. Some of these ferns are: hart's-tongue, southern maidenhair, walking fern, and cliff brakes.

Where to plant

- Besides the usual foundation planting on the north side of the house, plant ferns to fill in between and beneath shrubs.

- Grow them under grape arbors and in other shady spots.

Plant correctly

- Outdoor ferns should be planted in early fall for the best results.

❀ Some ferns grow with the crown above the soil; others grow with the crown below the soil. When planting a fern garden, be sure you know which type you have, for planting too deeply or too shallowly can damage or kill the plants.

❀ When transplanting ferns, cover them with a gallon jar to hold in the humidity and keep them from drying out. Leave the jar in place for about two weeks to let the roots become established, then remove it.

Fall and winter care

❀ Leave old fronds on outdoor ferns in fall. They help protect the plants in winter.

❀ Mulch ferns with leaves in late fall. In early spring, remove the mulch from the ferns by hand. Raking will damage the ferns. Leave the mulch around and between the ferns to conserve moisture.

Some to avoid

❀ Some ferns are invasive and should be avoided in the home garden unless you are prepared for a fight. These include bracken, hay-scented, sensitive and ostrich ferns.

Buy them

❀ Don't be tempted to collect ferns from the wild; many are protected species and even those that aren't may not survive the shock of moving. Better to buy your ferns, or if you're patient, collect spores and grow your own.

Good companions

❀ Wildflowers make the best companions for ferns. Most wildflowers like the same growing conditions as ferns, and they look nice together, since they are often partners in nature.

CHRISTMAS FERN

❀ Christmas fern is one of the best for the outdoor garden. It is both pretty and hardy.

❀ Christmas fern and Goldie's fern should be planted with the crowns above soil level.

❀ Christmas fern is good to grow on slopes. It does well, and will help retard erosion.

❀ If old Christmas fern fronds begin to look tattered, cut them off. It won't harm the plant.

GOLDIE'S FERN

❀ Goldie's wood fern, Christmas fern, oak fern, holly fern, fancy fern and maidenhair are a few that are good in gardens.

❀ Goldie's fern is the tallest wood fern, reaching to six feet. It should be planted at the back of the fern border or garden (with the crowns above soil level).

INTERRUPTED FERN

❀ The interrupted fern, *Osmunda claytoniana,* is one of the easiest to grow of the outdoor ferns, and is not particular about soil type.

MARGINAL SHIELD FERN

❀ Marginal shield fern and Christmas ferns do well when planted beneath pine trees.

NEW YORK FERN

❀ New York fern spreads rapidly and makes a good groundcover for a shady area, but may become invasive.

RUSTY WOODSIA FERN

❀ If you have a sunny spot where you want to grow ferns, try the rusty woodsia, *Woodsia ilvensis.* It prefers a sunny location.

10
Houseplants

Use the right pots

❀ For healthy houseplants, always use pots that have a drainage hole. If you have a pretty pot with no hole, either drill one in it, or pot your plant in a smaller, ordinary pot, and set the plain pot on top of some pebbles inside the pretty one.

Free pots

❀ A two-pound margarine bowl makes a colorful and attractive flower pot. Heat the point of an icepick in a flame, and melt a few drain holes in the bottom.

❀ Use a gallon-size plastic ice cream bucket to pot such large plants as cattleya orchids. Remember to cut several drain holes in the bottom first.

Get the pots ready

✼ Soak new clay pots in water overnight before using to keep the porous clay from drawing moisture from the soil of the newly potted plant.

✼ To keep from spreading diseases and insect pests, sterilize old flower pots by soaking overnight in a solution of one part Clorox to nine parts water.

Use the right soil

✼ A good potting mix for most houseplants is one part sand or perlite, one part peat and one part garden soil. Garden soil contains weed seeds and insects, so it should be sterilized before using. Put moist soil in a shallow pan and bake at 200° F. for one hour, stirring once after one-half hour. If you have a microwave, bake for fifteen minutes. Let the soil cool before using.

✼ If you have an old bean-bag chair that is ready for the junk man, save the filling. The tiny foam beads make an excellent soil additive. Use one part soil, one part peat, and one part foam beads for potting soil with good drainage. Besides providing drainage, the beads are very lightweight, so your potted plants will be easier to handle.

Add fresh soil

✼ If you have a tub plant such as a palm or ficus that is too large to repot easily, but needs fresh soil, scrape off the top two or three inches of soil and replace it with fresh.

Use good water

✼ Never use softened water for houseplants. The sodium content will accumulate in the soil and kill the plants.

✼ Put a large tub under the eaves of your house to catch rainwater for your houseplants. Add a few goldfish to get rid of mosquitoes. Rainwater is much better than city water with its chemicals, or country well water with its lime and rust.

Use fishy water

❀ When you change the water in your aquarium, save the old water and give it to your plants. The fish have added natural fertilizer to the water.

Don't overwater

❀ Most plants should not be watered until the soil feels dry. Stick your finger about an inch into the soil. If it feels dry, water thoroughly, let the water soak in, then water again. If water drains into the saucer, empty it within an hour.

Don't underwater

❀ Plants in clay pots need watering more often than those in plastic because clay is porous and lets the moisture evaporate. However, clay pots also let the plants' roots breathe, which is good, so it is a toss-up as to which type of pot is better.

Special water for special plants

❀ About once a month, water your acid-loving houseplants such as gardenias, citrus, etc., with leftover tea or coffee. Or use a solution of one teaspoon vinegar to one quart of water. All these add acidity to the soil.

Save your money

❀ Have you been tempted by the indoor hose advertised in garden magazines? This is the one you fasten to the faucet and use to water houseplants. Save your money! The hose is so small in diameter that the water flow is extremely slow. Whether you have a few houseplants or a hundred, it is faster and easier to water the old fashioned way, with a pitcher or watering can.

Conserve moisture

❀ If you use plastic pots instead of clay pots for your potted plants, you won't have to water as often. Be careful not to overwater.

❦ If you have a potted plant that dries out quickly, try the double-pot method of conserving moisture. Place the potted plant, pot and all, inside a larger pot. Pack moist peat moss between the pots. This will raise the humidity around the plant and keep the root ball moist longer.

When you're away

❦ Keep houseplants moist while you are away on vacation with a wick system. Put one end of the wick into a container of water and stick the other end about one inch into the pot's soil.

❦ Your plants will stay nicely moist for about three weeks if you put a layer of plastic on the bottom of the bathtub, then put several layers of newspaper on the plastic. Moisten the papers well, and set the plants in the tub. Tape a sheet of clear plastic over the tub to hold in the moisture.

❦ Or you can water each plant and slip the plant, pot and all, into a clear plastic bag. Close the bag. Set out of direct sun.

Change the water

❦ If you grow some houseplants in water, occasionally pour out the old water and refill with fresh, rather than just adding more. This is done for two reasons: to keep from harboring a breeding site for mosquitoes, and because mineral salts can build up in the water.

Houseplants need fertilizer

❦ It is a good idea to use two or three different brands of houseplant fertilizer and alternate them. Different fertilizers contain different micronutrients and in varying amounts, so if you use only one fertilizer, your plants may eventually be deprived of a necessary micronutrient. Another reason is that various fertilizers have different ratios of the three main nutrients, nitrogen, phosphorus, and potassium.

❀ Always moisten houseplants before fertilizing. Adding fertilizer to a dry root ball will burn the roots, damaging and sometimes even killing the plant.

Salts can build up

❀ A white crusty substance on the rim of a flowerpot indicates an accumulation of mineral salts from water or fertilizer. If allowed to build up, these salts are toxic to the plant. Remove the plant, and soak the pot in water overnight, then scrub with a stiff brush in hot water. Repot the plant, using fresh soil.

Provide light

❀ Provide extra light for houseplants by lining the shelf or window sill with aluminum foil. The soil reflects the light and the plants benefit.

Keep them straight

❀ Since plants grow toward the light source, potted plants in a window will soon stretch toward the window. To keep your plants growing straight, rotate the pots one-quarter turn each time you water them.

Light gardens need more care

❀ Plants grown under lights need to be watered and fertilized more often than those in window gardens, because these plants receive constant light, regardless of the season, and thus their growth is almost constant.

Turn off the lights

❀ If you grow plants under lights, turn the lights off at night. Plants, like people, need a nightly rest. An automatic timer is ideal for this job.

Replace the lights

✿ Plant lights should be replaced once a year, even though they still light. They gradually lose their strength, and the plants begin to stretch up, and stop blooming.

Raise the humidity

✿ A houseplant with browning tips on the leaves is probably suffering from a lack of humidity. Give it intensive care. Loop a wire over the plant as a frame, then slip a clear plastic bag over the wire, enclosing the plant. The bag will hold in the humidity and the plant should recover.

✿ Group your plants around the aquarium. The grouping is pretty and the aquarium raises the humidity around the plants.

✿ Group several plants together. The grouping creates its own little region of humidity.

✿ Set bowls of water among houseplants.

Use a free mister

✿ A window-cleaner spray bottle makes a good plant mister. Rinse it thoroughly before using.

Plants need air

✿ Don't crowd houseplants. You can group them together for better humidity, but give them enough room for good air circulation, which helps prevent disease and insect attacks.

Keep them clean

✿ Wash houseplants at least once a month to remove dust, which can clog the leaves' stomata (pores), and to keep insect pests away. Cover the soil with aluminum foil to keep it from washing out, and wash the plant in lukewarm water in the sink or shower. If the plant is too large to move, use a damp cloth to wash top and bottom sides of each leaf. Don't wash fuzzy-leaved plants such as gloxinia or African violets.

Don't shine them

❦ If you want healthy plants, don't use the spray leaf polish. Although shiny leaves may be pretty, the polish can clog the stomata, which makes it difficult for the plant to respire. Instead of shining, just keep the dust washed off. A little of the spray won't hurt, but most people tend to get carried away with the spray can.

Keep them warm

❦ On cold nights, slip a newspaper between potted plants and the window for extra protection against the chill.

Root-prune to maintain size

❦ To keep a plant at its present size, try root pruning. When the plant becomes rootbound (it will require watering very often and roots will protrude from the drain hole), knock the root ball from the pot. Use a sharp knife to slice off one inch of the bottom of the root ball and one-half inch around the sides. Put an inch of fresh soil in the same pot, replace the plant, and fill in around the sides with soil. Prune the tops to compensate for the root loss. Do not fertilize.

Plants for a north window

❦ You can have plants even in a cold north window, if you choose types that don't mind the cold, and there are many. A few foliage plants are: cultivars of English ivy, Boston fern, piggy back and strawberry begonia. Cyclamen, cineraria, calceolaria and primula are flowering plants that like it cool.

Look for insects

❦ When you buy houseplants, always check them carefully for insects. Although it is not common, a few greenhouses get rid of their insects by selling them with their plants. If you see any pests on the plants, it is better to buy them elsewhere. Most insects hide on the undersides of the leaves. Tiny white flying insects are white flies. Spider mites are very hard to see, but their damage is evident. They cause yellow or grey mottling of the foliage, and also make thin webs on the plant.

Aphids will be found on tender new growth. Aphids may be red, green, black or other colors. Scale insects are tiny and hard-shelled. They look almost like miniature turtles attached to the stems or near the leaf veins. Little wads of cotton in the leaf axils (where the leaf is attached to the stem) are not cotton at all, but mealy bugs, a real scourge.

Trap white flies

❧ White flies are attracted to yellow, so try coloring a dish of water with yellow food coloring and setting it among the plants. They will be attracted, and drown in the water.

❧ Or paint a piece of cardboard deep yellow and then dip it in motor oil. Hang it near the plants. The flies will get fatally stuck in the oil.

Use a flea collar

❧ Use a dog or cat flea collar to get rid of insect pests on houseplants. Lay the collar among the plants for a few days.

Screen them out

❧ Use a small square of aluminum-wire screen to cover the drain holes in flower pots. It prevents soil from washing out, and keeps slugs, sowbugs, and other insects from entering.

Get rid of mildew

❧ Once established on a plant, powdery mildew is very difficult to get rid of. If there are only a few spots (gray or white, fuzzy-looking), pick off and destroy the affected leaves. If the problem is more serious, the best answer is to get rid of the plant before the fungus disease spreads to other plants. Powdery mildew is caused by stale, moist air and too much water. Provide better ventilation or use a small fan to circulate the air, and cut down on the watering.

Keep cats out

❧ Use a generous sprinkling of pepper to keep your cat out of your potted plants. It is effective, without harming either cat or plants.

Make a pot trellis

❀ Make a small trellis for a vining plant from two pieces of wire. Use 11-gauge wire, which is about as heavy as a coat hanger. Cut two pieces, each about 36 inches long. If your plant is very large, you may want to make your trellis wires longer. Bend each wire into a horseshoe shape. Stick the ends of the first wire into the pot's soil. Crossing the wires at right angles, stick in the second wire. Train the plant up the trellis.

❀ Make a trellis from an old umbrella. Remove the cloth or plastic cover, open the umbrella frame and poke the handle in the soil near the plant.

❀ Make a totem pole for large vining plants. Using one-half-inch mesh hardware cloth, cut a piece from eight to ten inches wide, depending upon how large you want the pole's diameter, and as long as you want it, three feet or more. Roll the hardware cloth into a cylinder, fasten with wires and stuff it with moist, long-fiber sphagnum moss. Sink one end into the pot's soil and train the vine up the pole. When you water the plant, moisten the pole, and soon the plant will anchor itself into the pole.

Let them rest

❀ Most houseplants go semidormant in the low-light winter days. Allow them to have the rest they need. Water less frequently and do not fertilize at all. The exception to this rule is the plant that flowers continually such as African violets.

Protect your shelf

❀ Have a custom-fitted plant tray made to protect the flower shelf or window sill where your plants sit. Measure the length and width of the shelf. Have a sheet metal shop make the tray to these measurements, with a one-inch edge turned up on each side and end, and with the corners welded shut. Twenty-gauge galvanized steel is a good material to use. Add a coat of paint to match your decor, and you will have an attractive and useful addition to your window garden.

Move them easily

❀ To move large houseplants easily, place them on dollies. You can buy dolly-saucers, or make your own dollies with scrap boards and casters.

Make drip-proof hanging baskets

❀ You can make drip-proof baskets for indoor use from two-pound-size plastic margarine bowls (green is best to use with plants), some light-gauge wire, and five- or six-inch pots. Use a hot icepick to melt four holes equidistant around the bowls. Make the holes about one-half inch below the rims. Now cut two pieces of wire 40 inches long, for each basket. Bend each in half. To make the hanging hook, lay the two pieces together and twist the bent ends around each other a few times. Curve to form a hook. Bend up the four opposite ends about two inches from the ends. Set the pot, planted with a vine or other trailing plant, in the bowl. Stick the four ends of wire into the four holes and twist once to secure. No more dripping on the carpet when you water your indoor hanging baskets.

Make a coconut basket

❀ Make a cute hanging basket for a small trailing plant from a coconut. Use a saw to cut off a small portion of the end opposite the three eyes. Remove the meat. Drill three small holes equidistant around the cut edge and insert hanging wires. Poke a drain hole through one of the eyes. Fill with potting soil and add a small plant.

Make a hanging rod

❀ Use an old broomstick or mop handle to make a hanging rod for your hanging baskets. Cut off the broom or mop; paint the handle. Screw two sturdy hooks into the porch or patio roof, placing them not quite as far apart as the handle is long. Suspend the rod with two equal lengths of dog chain. This rod will hold two to four hanging baskets, depending on their size.

Hanging baskets need watering often

❀ Check plants in hanging baskets daily in the summer to see if they need watering. Wind and sun dry hanging baskets much more quickly than other containers.

�֍ Hanging baskets on high beams or high on the wall look nice, but are a nuisance when it is time to water them. Make this chore easier by rigging up a rope and pulley system so each basket can be lowered to a convenient height for watering.

Summer houseplants outside

✖ If your houseplants spend the summer outside, provide a sheltered spot for them. Set four ten-foot wooden posts about two and one-half feet into the ground. Connect the posts by nailing 1 × 3 boards to their tops. Buy greenhouse shade cloth and stretch it over the top and around three sides of the shelter, stapling it to the posts and boards. The plastic shade cloth will allow rain and filtered sun to reach the plants, but will protect them from wind and hail.

✖ Houseplants summering outdoors won't blow off their perches if you make a special shelf for them. Measure the rim diameter of each pot, then cut a hole in the shelf for each pot approximately one-half inch smaller than the pot's diameter. Mount the shelf and set the pots into the holes. They will be secure even in a summer storm.

✖ Most houseplants benefit from a summer outdoors (the exceptions are the fuzzy-leaf plants). A houseplant tree is an attractive way to display the shade-loving varieties. Drive nails in a spiral fashion into the tree trunk, and use the hangers described in the next hint to hang the pots. Wind can't overturn the plants, and the tree's foliage will protect them from hard rains and hot sun.

Bring them inside

✖ Houseplants may go into shock and drop many of their leaves when brought back inside after summering outdoors. Minimize the shock by bringing them in gradually. Start at least two weeks before the first expected frost date. Move the plants from full sun to partial shade for a few days, then to full shade for a few more days. Finally move them inside while it is still warm enough to have the windows open. Plants acclimatized in this manner will suffer much less than those moved abruptly to the dim light and hot dry air in most homes.

❧ Before bringing the plants inside, take a look at the pots' drain holes. Slugs, snails, sowbugs, centipedes and other pests may be hiding there to hitch a ride inside.

❧ Check plants for aphids, scale, white flies and other pests before bringing them inside. Spray if you see any.

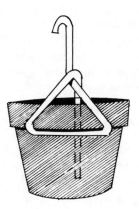

Make free pot hangers

❧ Make handy pot hangers out of wire coat hangers. Cut a piece of wire about 16 inches long from the hanger. Use pliers to bend a small hook in one end for hanging. About an inch down from the hook, form an angle of about 135°. Two and one-half inches from this angle, make a 45° angle in the opposite direction. Then three and one-half inches from the second angle, make another 45° angle to form a small triangle. Bend the extra wire around the hanging hook, so that it is pointing straight down. This wire is inserted into the soil at the pot's edge. The base of the triangle is hooked under the pot's rim. The weight of the clay pot (not larger than 5 inches) against the triangle keeps the pot securely in place.

Multiply your houseplants

❧ Always use a clean sharp knife to take cuttings for propagation. Scissors can mash plant cells and cause the cuttings to rot.

Try Grandma's way

For propagating only a few cuttings in a flower pot, an idea from Grandma's day is still a good one. Turn a glass jar upside down over the cuttings to hold in humidity and prevent wilt. They should root more quickly.

Bags are good containers

Large clear plastic bags make good containers for propagating cuttings. Put about three inches of moist potting soil, vermiculite or sand in the bottom of the bag. Stick in the cuttings, close the bag, and put in a warm bright spot out of direct sunlight. The bag keeps in humidity, keeps cuttings warm and eliminates the need to water.

Use a rooting hormone

Dip the ends of cuttings into a rooting hormone powder before sticking in the rooting medium, for better results.

Water isn't as good

Success is more likely in propagating plants by leaf cuttings if the leaves are stuck in moist sand or vermiculite instead of rooting them in water. Cuttings rooted in water often go into shock and die when potted in soil. Cuttings rooted in a solid medium don't suffer such shock when transplanted, and more will survive.

Keep the medium evenly moist

The most frequent reason for failure in attempts to propagate plants with cuttings is improper watering. If overwatered, they rot. If underwatered, they dry up. Eliminate this problem by using the double pot method. Fill a large pot with vermiculite or sand. Make a hole in the center and into the hole place a small clay pot whose drain hole has been plugged with a cork. Plastic pots won't work. Fill the center pot with water, adding more as the water level lowers. Stick the cuttings in the medium between the two pots. Moisture will slowly soak through the porous sides of the small pot into the medium, keeping it just right for inducing the cuttings to root.

Leaf cuttings

✣ Plants such as African violets and gloxinias can be easily propagated by leaf cuttings. Cut off a medium-size leaf with about one inch of stem attached. Stick in rooting hormone powder, shake off the excess, and stick into the rooting medium. Other plants, such as schefflera, should have the entire petiole (leaf stem) left on. Snap this off the plant, then dip and stick.

Stem cuttings

✣ The length of stem cuttings depends on the size of the plant. Cut right at a node. There should be one or two sets of leaves on the cutting, not counting those right at the cut. Remove this pair of leaves, and also remove any flowers or buds, to hasten rooting. You may be able to get several cuttings from a single length of stem. Dip in hormone powder and stick into rooting medium, being sure to stick them right side up. An upside-down cutting will die.

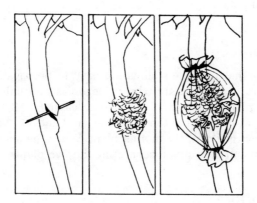

Air-layering

✣ Plants with thick stems, such as rubber plants, dieffenbachias and ti plants may be propagated by air-layering. Make a cut, slanted upward, two-thirds of the way through the stem, cutting at a node. Prop the stem wound open with a toothpick. Dust lightly with rooting hormone powder. Pack moist sphagnum moss, the long-fibered kind, around and into the wound. Wrap the moss with clear plastic to keep the moisture in, and seal at the top and bottom of the plastic with tape. When you see roots growing in the moss, cut the new plant from the old. New leaves will sprout from the old stem, and you will now have two plants.

Leaf section cuttings

Sanseveria and Rex begonias can be started from leaf-section cuttings. Sanseveria is simple. Cut a leaf into three inch sections, dip in hormone powder and stick into rooting medium. An easy way to tell which end should be up is to cut a V-shaped notch in the top of each as you cut the leaf. The Rex begonia is a bit more complicated. Cut most of the stem from the leaf, but leave about one-eighth inch of it attached. Cut the leaf into wedge-shaped sections, making sure each section has a portion of the stem and at least two large veins. Stick the stem end about one-half inch into a rooting medium. When the new leaves are about one-half inch in diameter, carefully separate the plantlets, and plant them in small individual pots.

Stolons

Plants that produce stolons are easy to propagate. Some of these are episcias, strawberry begonias and chlorophytum. Put a plantlet in a small pot of soil, leaving it attached to the mother plant. Curve the runner around and set the small pot in the large pot of the mother plant. When the plantlet is well rooted, cut the runner, separating the two plants.

ALOE VERA

Grow a medicine plant

Grow an *Aloe vera* as a living first-aid kit. These attractive succulent plants have been popular for years as a source of quick relief for minor burns, insect bites, poison ivy and other skin irritations. Snap off a piece of a leaf and rub the jellylike juice on the irritation. It soothes the pain and seems to promote healing. Plant aloe in a mix of half sand and half soil. Water only when the soil feels dry, and place in a sunny window.

AMARYLLIS
Use a small pot

❀ Amaryllis bulbs may not bloom if they are in too large a pot. There should be no more than one inch of space on each side of the bulb. At least one-third of the bulb should be above the soil line.

Don't let seeds form

❀ Always cut off the faded flowers of your amaryllis so no seeds form. Producing seeds robs the bulb of strength that should go to next year's flowers.

Treat them right

❀ To get amaryllis bulbs to bloom again, feed and water them regularly until September, then stop watering to give them a rest. In December, water once. When you see buds forming, resume watering. As growth starts, begin feeding.

AFRICAN VIOLETS
Use small pots

❀ African violets do well when potted in rather small pots. A good general rule is to use a pot one-third the diameter of the plant.

Make them bloom

❀ Encourage African violets to bloom by giving them plenty of light. They can be in a south window during dark winter months. They bloom beautifully under fluorescent lights. In fact, they seem to prefer them. They should be fertilized every watering at one-fourth strength. Water from the top, to prevent salt buildup in the soil, but avoid wetting the leaves,

which can cause spots. Once every month or so, water
thoroughly with plain water to leach any accumulated salts
from the soil.

Renew an old plant

❀ If your old African violet has a bare ugly stem, cut the plant
off about two inches below the lower leaves. Dip the cut end
in rooting hormone powder and then pot in coarse vermiculite
or soilless mix. Keep moist but not soggy. The stem will soon
root, and you will have a much more attractive plant.

AVOCADO
Plant a seed

❀ Remove an avocado pit from the fruit and wrap it in a moist
paper towel. Place in a plastic bag and close the bag. Lay it in
a warm place. Check every few days to see if the towel needs
to be moistened. When roots appear, plant in potting soil for a
pretty houseplant.

BEGONIA
Begonias rot easily

❀ Most dying begonias are victims of rot. Plant with the crown
slightly above soil level. Water only when the soil feels dry,
watering less during the winter months.

BROMELIADS
Bromeliads are easy

❀ Grow a bromeliad if you want a houseplant that is practically
care-free. Pot it in a loose mixture of soil, sand, and bark,
equal parts; set it in a sunny window and keep water in its
center, which is formed into a natural vase. Fill the vase with
water and you can forget it for two or three weeks until it is
time for a refill. Bromeliads are available with beautiful foliage varying in color from silver gray to purple-striped, and
the brilliantly colored blooms of many bromeliads will last for
months.

Share a banana with your bromeliads

❧ Eat your banana and feed the peel to your bromeliads. Bromeliads benefit from the phosphorus the peels contain. Cut the peel in small pieces and drop it in the center of the plant, in its natural vase. Occasionally replace the old peel with fresh.

Make them bloom

❧ Mature bromeliads can be tricked into blooming. Put the plant, pot and all, in a large clear plastic bag and place a very ripe apple in the bag with it. Close the bag. The apple will give off ethylene gas, which may induce the bromeliad to bloom. Leave the apple and plant in the bag for about a week.

CACTI AND SUCCULENTS
Avoid the stickers

❧ If you don't like stickers in your fingers, hold cacti with kitchen tongs as you repot them.

Use the right potting mix

❧ Do not pot cacti in plain sand, or they won't grow. They may survive, but that is all, because sand contains no nutrients. Use a mixture of one part sand and one part soil.

❧ Most desert cacti need a bit of lime or crushed eggshells in the potting soil.

❧ If you can't get sand for your cacti, substitute bird gravel, available at pet stores.

Pot them right

❧ Pot cacti in small pots if you want flowers. Most begin to bloom sooner if rootbound.

❧ To pot a cactus or succulent, fill the bottom fourth of the pot with pot shards or gravel for good drainage, sprinkle on a layer of activated charcoal (*not* from briquets, which are toxic to plants), then add an inch or so of the potting mix described above, with a little lime or eggshell added. Hold the cactus at the proper level in the pot and fill in with more soil mix. Don't water yet. Wait about four days to keep the roots from rotting.

Water correctly

❀ Water when the soil feels dry in the summer months. Cut down in the winter when the cacti are semidormant. Water only enough to keep them from shriveling.

❀ Epiphyllums (orchid cacti) need more water than most cacti. This takes experience. Keep the soil moist. If they start to rot, cut them off, reroot in sand, and try again with less water.

Feed sparingly

❀ Cacti and succulents may be fertilized every six months with soluble houseplant fertilizer, at half strength. Feed in February and August.

Give the proper light

❀ Cacti may suffer from sunburn if moved outdoors to full sun after being used to the dim indoor light. Put them in light shade at first, then gradually increase the amount of sun they receive.

❀ Desert cacti need more sun and less water than the epiphytic cacti.

❀ Christmas cactus is a short-day plant. This means that in order to set flower buds, it must have at least twelve hours per day of uninterrupted darkness starting in mid-October. Either grow it in an unused room where no lights will be turned on (not even once) or cover it with a grocery bag every evening at six and uncover at seven or so every morning till you see buds forming. Grow in a cool spot.

Let it rest

❀ Peanut cactus, *Chamaecereus silvestrii,* needs a winter rest period in a cold place, at 35°–40° F.

Start from pups or cuttings

❀ Start more cacti from pups or cuttings, which are treated the same. A pup is merely an offset from the parent plant. Cut it off, or take a cutting. Lay aside for a few days to allow the wound to dry and heal. This keeps it from rotting. Then stick in clean moist sand in a warm, brightly lit place out of direct sun. Don't overwater. When roots form, plant in small pots in cactus potting mix.

FREESIAS
Freesias are deliciously fragrant

❀ Plant freesia bulbs in September for fragrant winter blooms. Put about eight of the small bulbs in an eight-inch pot. Plant with the tips showing above the soil. Water and place in a sunny window. Fertilize with soluble houseplant fertilizer when they are two or three inches tall.

FUCHSIA
Wake them up in February

❀ Start watering and fertilizing indoor fuchsias in February to break dormancy. Pinch out the tips at least twice to make them branch for a more compact plant and more flowers. They like a cool window.

GERANIUM
Store for the winter

❀ An easy way to store geraniums through the winter is to remove them from the soil and place them in a box between layers of newspaper. Store in a cool dry room. In early spring, plant in pots, set in a cool, bright window, and water lightly. These will not start blooming as quickly as those grown in pots all winter.

GARDENIA
Keep corsages longer

❀ Cut when only half-open to prolong the life of a gardenia to be used in a corsage. Place in lukewarm water in a clean vase, let sit an hour, then cover with a plastic bag and set in the refrigerator till ready to use.

Gardenias need cool nights

❀ Gardenias must have a night temperature of no more than 62° F. if they are to set flower buds. They also need plenty of sunshine and an acid soil. Use peat in the mix to add acidity.

HOYA
Make them bloom

❀ If hoyas (wax plants) won't bloom, try potting them in small pots, in coarse vermiculite. Keep the humidity around them as high as possible, and be sure they get plenty of light.

❀ After the flowers have fallen from your hoyas, never remove the bloom spurs because in all but the *H. bella,* hoyas bloom year after year from the same spurs.

PHILODENDRON
Make the split leaf split

❀ If your split-leaf philodendron's new leaves are not split, this means it is not getting the growing conditions it needs. Mist daily to improve humidity, move to a spot where it receives more light, and keep the soil constantly moist, but not soggy. Fertilize during spring and summer with soluble houseplant fertilizer.

POINSETTIA
Keep it blooming

❀ If green shoots appear at the flower of your blooming poinsettia, remove them. The red bracts will last much longer.

SENSITIVE PLANT
Grow some fun

❀ Plant seeds of *Mimosa pudica* or sensitive plant to delight your favorite child. Sow in sterile potting soil, keep warm and moist. When the seedlings appear, put in a south window. Sensitive plants snap their leaves shut and droop their leaf stems when touched, but soon recover, ready to do it all over again.

STRAWBERRY
Plant a strawberry basket

❀ For an unusual houseplant, pot up three strawberry plants in a hanging basket. They are pretty trailing plants, with their runners cascading over the edge of the basket, and you may be rewarded with a few delicate white blossoms and out-of-season berries.

TI
Sprout a ti log

❀ Ti plants are pretty and easy to grow. They come in a surprising variety of foliage colors: pale green, dark green, purple, red, and stripes of green and cream, green and pink, etc. If you buy a ti log to start your plant, it will probably be covered with paraffin to help keep it from drying out. Scrape off as much of the paraffin as you can, but be sure you don't damage any buds popping through. If you can't tell which end is up, don't take chances: An upside down cutting won't grow, so lay the log on its side in a shallow bowl and keep it half submerged in water till it sprouts roots and leaves. Then you can either pot it in soil or continue to grow it in water, adding a little gravel for anchorage.

VINES
Grow some curtains

❀ Replace your old kitchen curtains with living curtains. Plant vines such as grape ivy, three to a pot. Set a pot at each end of the window sill. Screw cup hooks into the window trim, and train the vines to grow around the window, fastening them to the cup hooks with wire twist-ties. Your kitchen will be much brighter, for the vines will let in more sunlight than curtains do.

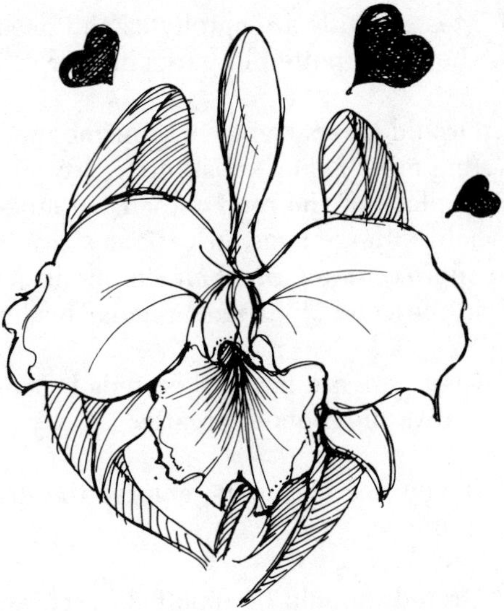

11

Orchids

Choose what is right for you

- Choose orchids according to the amount of warmth you can supply them. Warm growers such as phalaenopsis need a night temperature of 60° to 70° F. Intermediates such as cattleyas, laelias, and oncidiums need night temperatures of 55° to 60° F. Cool growers such as miltonias, cymbidiums and dendrobiums need night temperatures of 50° to 55° F.

Start with the easy ones

- Cattleya, laelia and phalaenopsis, and oncidiums are some of the easiest for the beginner to grow.

- Cymbidiums do not make good houseplants because they need more light and cooler temperatures than most homes can supply.

Potting and repotting orchids

✻ Most orchids are epiphytes and need perfect drainage. They should be potted in bark chips or osmunda fiber.

✻ Orchid lovers can save some money when buying orchid potting mix, if they substitute redwood chips sold for mulching, in place of the more expensive mix. The redwood chips are sold in large bags, in various sizes. Buy the small-size chips, approximately one-half- to one-inch pieces. Orchids planted in redwood chips need regular feeding.

✻ Clay pots are best for orchids because their porous material allows the roots to breathe.

✻ If you use clay pots, enlarge the drain hole to allow faster drainage.

✻ Orchids should be repotted every two years in fresh bark or fiber, because if not replaced the medium breaks down and hampers drainage.

✻ The best time to repot most orchids is when new roots are starting to grow, just when they are barely visible as "bumps" on the orchid's base.

✻ Long roots may be broken during repotting, so trim them back to four inches.

✻ Repot cymbidiums after flowering.

Watering orchids

✻ Many orchids have thickened stems called pseudobulbs. The pseudobulbs store water. Plants with pseudobulbs don't need to be watered as often as those without. Wait until the potting medium is dry before watering. Overwatering causes the roots to rot. If leaves begin to shrivel, even though the potting medium is moist, as sometimes happens in hot weather, mist the plant daily.

❧ Water orchids in the sink. Stand the pot in lukewarm water up to its rim till thoroughly soaked. Let drain and return to the window. Never let water sit in the saucer.

❧ Do not water orchids for about two weeks after repotting them. Instead, mist daily. Mist in the morning so the leaves will be dry by nightfall (wet leaves at night encourage fungus attack). Start watering when you see new roots growing.

❧ Paphiopedilums should be kept moist. Pot in bark and water frequently.

❧ Most oncidiums need less water in fall and winter, when they are semidormant.

Give them light

❧ Most orchids need as much light as is possible without burning the leaves.

❧ Cattleyas can be grown in a south window in winter, an east window in summer, in most parts of the country.

❧ Dendrobiums need full sun. Temperature requirements vary according to the species.

Feeding them

❧ Orchids planted in bark need fertilizing more often than those planted in osmunda.

❧ Yellow leaves indicate the plants need more fertilizer, dark green leaves indicate they need more light. Healthy leaves should be grass green for most types of orchids.

Don't spread disease

❧ Sterilize your knife in flame before each cut to prevent spreading fungus diseases when dividing orchid plants.

CATTLEYAS
They like to summer outside

❀ Cattleyas, laelias, oncidiums and dendrobiums benefit from a summer vacation outdoors in light shade or in a sunny spot.

CYMBIDIUMS
They can be difficult

❀ Cymbidiums need plenty of light, warm days of from 70° to 80° F., and cool nights of 45° to 50° F. to set flower buds.

Cymbidiums are terrestrial

❀ Cymbidiums are terrestrial and should be potted in a soil mix of equal parts garden soil, compost and bark.

DENDROBIUMS
Use small pots

❀ Dendrobium root systems are small, so use small pots. If the plant is top heavy, set the small pot inside a larger one for stability.

Some need a rest

❀ Some of the deciduous dendrobiums need a cool dry rest in fall and early winter to induce flowering.

PHALAENOPSIS
Phalaenopsis make good beginner's orchids

❀ Phalaenopsis need indirect light, night temperatures of 60° to 68° F. and more frequent watering than cattleyas, since they have no pseudobulbs.

Feed them

❀ Phalaenopsis need to be fed at least every two weeks with an orchid fertilizer.

Keep them inside

❀ They should not be summered outdoors.

Make them bloom again

❀ Phalaenopsis will often bloom again if you cut back by one-third the bloom spike when the flowers fade. Cut just above a node, and the spike will branch, producing more flowers.

12

Pests and Animal Friends

Keep the rabbits and raccoons away

❧ Sprinkle lettuce and cabbages with red pepper to ruin the appetites of nibbling rabbits. Repeat after each rain.

❧ If small animals are helping themselves to the best of your garden, try this trick to keep them away. Visit the nearest zoo and ask the caretaker for some of the manure from animals such as lions and tigers. Spread it thinly throughout the garden. Fresh manure can burn plants, so do not let it touch the plants, and do spread it very thinly. No self-respecting rabbit or raccoon will come near a garden that smells of lions and tigers.

❧ Never put your dog on a leash or chain in the garden to keep raccoons out of the corn rows. Tethered in this way he will be helpless against two or three large coons. They may even kill him. You *can* put some dog-scented straw from his house out along the rows.

❦ Try planting pumpkins all around the outside of the corn patch to keep animals out. The animals don't like to cross the prickly vines.

Protect your bird feeder from squirrels

❦ Use a plastic jug to stop squirrels from raiding your pole-mounted bird feeder. Cut the bottom from a gallon jug and slip it up the pole, about three-fourths of the way up, right side up. Drill a hole through the pole and the top of the jug, and fasten with wire. The squirrels won't be able to get past the jug.

Get the birds to help

❦ Get rid of mosquitoes from your yard with a safe and entertaining mosquito destroyer, the purple martin. You can attract martins by providing housing for them, and you can grow the houses. Grow birdhouse gourds. In the fall, harvest them and let them dry in a warm airy place. When they are completely dry, cut a circle two and one-fourth inches in diameter in each, for a door. Cut a small hole in the bottom to drain any rain that gets in. Make holes in the neck for a hanging wire. No perch is necessary. Martins are communal birds, so make several houses and hang them in a group in a fairly open space at a height of about fifteen feet.

❦ To help control insects in the fruit and vegetable garden, set up bird feeders to lure birds to the area. They will help themselves to some of your produce, but they deserve a little dessert for all the insects and weed seeds they eat.

Try nature's way

❦ If you see a snake in your lawn or garden, let him go. Most snakes are not only harmless, but are actually helpful because they eat insects and small rodents.

❀ Marigolds are valuable in the vegetable garden. They help deter bean beetles and other insects, as well as nematodes.

❀ Trichogramma is a parasitic wasp that attacks cabbage worms, corn earworms, tomato hornworms, cut worms, and other pests. Buy eggs and apply in your garden three times, two weeks apart, for good control. They are available from seed catalogs.

❀ If you see a tomato hornworm with little white things attached to its back, don't kill it. It is already dying, and by letting it alone, you will help to kill many more of the pests. The white things are cocoons of the parasitic braconid wasp. The wasp lays its eggs in the hornworm. The larvae feed on the worm and then pupate on its back till mature.

❀ Treating your lawn with milky spore disease is effective against Japanese beetles. It won't harm pets or people.

❀ The praying mantis is one of the gardener's best friends. Buy mantis egg cases, or hunt for them along country roadsides. They are about the size of a walnut, tan, and are made of a tough plasticlike foam. Tie the cases to rose canes and on stakes throughout the vegetable garden. They should be about two feet above the ground. The mantises provide natural insect control, and will not harm people, despite their ferocious appearance.

Ladybugs may fly away home

❀ You may see ladybugs advertised for sale as natural control against insect pests. While it is true they are very beneficial, you shouldn't waste your money on them, because they are territorial creatures and when you release them in the garden, most will fly away in search of their own territory. You may be providing a help to your neighbor's garden, however!

Wash pests away

❀ Use a hard spray of water from the garden hose to wash aphids, spider mites and other insect pests from outdoor plants. Repeat every few days until the pests are under control. Indoor plants may be given the same treatment in the kitchen sink or shower.

Killing weeds the easy way

❀ If you have persistent weeds, such as poison ivy, that cultivation (with a rakelike cultivator or a spading fork) doesn't seem to kill, try smothering them with black plastic. In late fall, spread sheets of plastic over the problem area and anchor with bricks or stones. The weeds should all be gone by the next spring when you remove the plastic.

❀ To kill grass and weeds growing through cracks in patios, garden walks or driveways, pour boiling water on them.

❀ An easy way to edge the lawn around walks or patios is to pour salt in a narrow strip over grass alongside them. This is effective for several weeks.

❀ In flower gardens, a three-inch layer of grass clippings can be used as a mulch that will help soil retain moisture, add nutrients, *and* eliminate most weeds.

Knocking out slugs

❀ Kill slugs and snails without poison. Make a shallow hole in the soil and set a saucer in it, with the rim of the saucer level with the soil. Fill the saucer with beer. Since they love beer, the slugs and snails will crawl in and drown. Refill the saucer each evening.

❀ Lay boards in the garden or flower bed. The next morning, turn the boards over and you will find slugs hiding under them. To kill the slugs, sprinkle with salt.

❀ Put wood ashes around plants to keep slugs away.

❀ If you have slugs in your greenhouse, put out some slices of potato for them in the evening. Early the next morning, go to the greenhouse and catch them at the lure. Use salt on them or pitch them out in the cold.

Cutting out cutworms

❧ Put a four-inch-high cardboard collar around young plants to keep cutworms away. Shove it into the soil about one inch, since they also hide under the soil.

Beating the beetles

❧ Pick off Mexican bean beetles and drop in a can of water mixed with kerosene to kill them.

❧ Lure Japanese beetles away from your potato plants by planting borage around the potato patch. They prefer the borage, and though some will find the potatoes, most will stay in the borage border.

Sugar blues

❧ Nematodes don't like sugar. Sprinkle at a rate of one pound per fifty feet of row in rows of susceptible plants at planting time to control these minute worm pests.

Save your squash

❧ Plant radishes among your squashes to help prevent borers. Don't harvest the radishes. Let them remain to do their job.

❧ You can also control borers by sprinkling wood ashes on the soil around the squash at planting time.

❧ Another squash bug deterrent is aluminum foil. Use it as a mulch under the vines. The bugs don't like the reflected light.

Pests in trees

❧ Watch for bagworm egg cases in evergreens, sycamores and maples during fall and winter. The bags are about two inches long, pointed at top and bottom, and are covered with small twigs or dried needles. They hang from the branches and are fairly easily seen. Pick them off and burn them.

❧ Holes with gummy blobs and "sawdust" in peach and cherry trees indicate borers. Poke a wire in the holes to kill the pests.

❀ At the first sight of tent caterpillars (you will notice gauzy tents in the branches of trees) spread an old sheet under any infested tree. Make a torch with a kerosene-soaked rag wired to a pole. Burn as much of the web and worms as possible. Many of the worms will drop off onto the sheet, still alive. Destroy them by squashing or fold them up into the sheet and burn the whole bundle.

❀ In late winter, look for tent-caterpillar eggs on branches of fruit trees. The egg masses are blue black. Remove them now to prevent a lot of damage in the warm season.

Get rid of houseplant pests

❀ If you see insects on your houseplants, but are out of bug spray, zap them with hairspray or spray starch. It smothers the pests, but will flake off before it damages the plants.

❀ A safe insecticide for houseplants is one-fourth cup Ivory liquid to one gallon of water. Spray on plants.

❀ If you see a few mealybugs (they look like fluffs of cotton) on your plants, touch each with a cotton swab soaked in nail polish remover or alcohol. If there are too many of the pests for this method, isolate the infested plant and spray with a mixture of one part alcohol and one part water. Or it may be best to burn the plant quickly before the little monsters spread to your other plants.

Don't leave fallen rose leaves

❀ Fallen rose and peony leaves may harbor disease and insect pests over the winter if allowed to remain on the ground. Clean them up in late autumn and burn them. Don't take chances by adding them to the compost pile.

Make your own duster

❀ Save money when buying all-purpose garden dust. Instead of buying it in a sprinkler can, buy it by the bag, and make your own sprinkler. All you have to do is poke some holes in the plastic lid of a roasted-nut can, potato chip can or coffee can.

Fill with dust, and then tape the lid on with masking tape to make sure it doesn't come off as you sprinkle your plants.

Use two sprayers

❧ You should have two sprayers if you spray herbicides and insecticides. Use one only for herbicides, the other only for insecticides. Label them so there is no danger of a mixup. No matter how well you clean the herbicide sprayer, you may get some plant damage if it is used later for spraying insecticide.

Add a "sticker"

❧ Add a squirt of Ivory liquid to your sprayer when preparing to use an insecticide. The soap will make the droplets of spray cling to the plant, instead of immediately dripping off. Ivory is recommended because it is a soap, not a detergent.

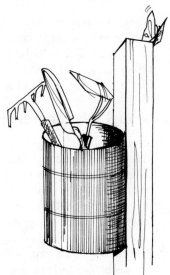

13

Tools, Techniques and Other Garden Wisdom

Use your window wells as cold frames

❧ Use your basement window wells for handy cold frames. Just cover with clear or white fiberglass and seal around the edges. Do your watering from the basement to prevent heat loss.

Compost your vegetable scraps

❧ Make a temporary compost bin from a large cardboard box lined with a plastic leaf bag. Get a big box from a TV or appliance store. Start with an eight-inch layer of vegetable matter such as grass clippings, leaves, and kitchen waste, then add a two-inch layer of soil and a two-inch layer of manure. Repeat the layers until the box is full. Keep moist, but not soggy. Stir with a potato fork about every three weeks. Soon you will have rich compost to use in your garden.

Another quick and easy way to make a compost bin is to use a large plastic garbage can. Drill some holes in the sides for air circulation. Fill with layers of shredded garden and kitchen refuse, soil, and manure. Moisten, but don't keep it soggy. Cover with the lid so rain won't leach out the nutrients.

Save fuel in your greenhouse

Save about 40 percent of the cost of fuel to heat your greenhouse. Line it with a layer of plastic, in addition to its original covering. If the greenhouse has a wood frame, the plastic can be stapled to the frame. If the frame is metal, use bubble plastic and apply to the glass like wallpaper. Don't use paste; plain water will make the plastic stick to the glass.

Barrels of water can help heat your greenhouse. Paint the barrels black, and place them where they can absorb the sun's heat during the day. The heat will be slowly released at night, cutting the fuel bill. Be sure to seal the barrels to avoid a constant supply of mosquitoes.

Information helps

Seed catalogs contain a wealth of information on hundreds of varieties of flowers, vegetables, fruit trees and other plants. Send for some and study them for a pleasurable winter pastime, and to learn the growing requirements for the many different kinds of plants you may want to try in your garden.

Check a hardiness-zone map before planting flowering perennials, trees, shrubs, etc. There is no sense wasting time and money in planting kinds that are not hardy in your zone. Zone maps can be found in many seed catalogs.

Many gardeners tend to think that planting according to the almanac is akin to consulting a witch doctor, but old-timers as well as scientists agree that it works. Get an almanac and follow it for a super garden.

Mulch: Use it with care

Mulching between plants in the vegetable or flower garden saves much work. A mulch conserves moisture, smothers weeds and keeps the soil at a more constant temperature. Organic mulch such as leaves or straw will also improve the soil when it eventually breaks down.

🎋 If you use fresh grass clippings as a mulch, make sure they don't touch your plants. As they decompose, they give off sufficient heat to burn plants.

🎋 Don't use pine needles as a general garden mulch. The needles contain tannin, which is toxic to many plants. They are okay for acid-loving plants, though.

🎋 Maple leaves make a poor winter mulch for protecting plants. When wet they get soggy and compacted, and can smother the plants. Oak leaves are better because they won't get so compressed.

🎋 In fall, remove plant debris from the garden. It is a perfect hiding place for insects and diseases to spend the winter. Put it on the compost pile. A hot working compost will kill the pests.

Pools add beauty

🎋 You can build a small pool for goldfish and water plants in an afternoon. Choose a site that will receive several hours of sun each day to keep the plants healthy, but with afternoon shade so you can sit comfortably by the pool to enjoy the fish and flowers. Dig a hole the size you want the pool to be. If you want a standard water lily, the hole should be at least 24 inches deep. Miniature lilies and other water plants can be grown in shallower pools. Remove any sharp stones, and line the hole with a large sheet of heavy plastic. Place bricks or stones on the edges of the sheet to anchor it and also to hide part of the plastic. Fill with water and add the fish and plants. Plant lilies or bog plants in tubs or pots of soil. Cover the soil with an inch of sand to prevent clouding the water when you submerge them. Standard lilies should have at least fifteen inches of water over the crowns. Many kinds of water plants are available, and most have pretty flowers. You don't need to feed the fish; they will eat algae and mosquito larvae. This little pool will give you hours of pleasure.

❧ If you have a large frog living at your fish pool, it is best to find him another home. Frogs will eat anything that moves, and is small enough to get in their mouths. This includes your small goldfish. Small frogs will do no damage.

❧ When winter comes, put a short section of a log in your pool. The ice will push up on the log as the pool freezes, instead of out on the sides of the pool, helping to prevent cracking.

Two unusual planters

❧ Featherrock, a porous, lightweight rock available at many garden centers, makes an unusual and a very pretty planter for sempervivums and small creeping sedums. Chisel a planting hole in the rock, fill with soil and add the plants.

❧ To get a lot of use from a small sunny space, or just for something unusual, try building a block garden. Set a cement block with the holes up, on a level surface. It should be in full sun for best growing. Cut both ends out of a small can such as a soup can, and set it in the center of one of the holes. Fill the can with gravel, and fill in around it with soil. Remove the can and repeat in the other hole. Plant two petunias or other plants in each hole. Put in plants to lie horizontally (roots in soil, not gravel). Lay a wooden block, one inch thick, on each corner of the cement block, to allow room for the plants. Lay the second block on top and repeat the procedure until your block garden is about seven blocks high. Water from the top. The gravel in the center of each hole helps the water to reach the lower blocks. This is a pretty planter that needs only a minimum space, but check often to see if it needs water as the small planting holes dry out rather quickly.

Move heavy planters easily

❧ Use a wide blade shovel to move a heavy planter. Push the shovel blade under the planter, and then pull to slide the planter to its new location.

❧ Another way to move heavy planters is to use three pieces of pipe to roll them. Tip up the planter and put two of the pipes under it, several inches apart. Roll the planter till it is nearly

off the rear roller, then place the third roller under the planter in front. Keep rolling, replacing the rear roller in front, until the planter is where you want it.

Get soil ready

❀ An easy test to see if the garden soil is workable is to squeeze a handful. If it forms a ball, it is too wet. If it falls apart into two or three clumps, it is just right. If it all falls entirely apart, it is dry.

❀ Warm soil for early plantings in spring by spreading black plastic over the area to be planted. The plastic will absorb the sun's heat. Leave the plastic in place for a few days, then remove and plant the seeds.

❀ Peat and soilless mixes are difficult to moisten. Use warm water, because it will soak in more easily than cold water.

❀ Don't be tempted by the low price to buy black peat. This is sold by weight at discount stores, and even at garden centers, where they should know better. Black peat does more harm to plants than good. It keeps soil soggy and drowns plants because it is so fine that it fills up the soil's natural air spaces. Buy the brown peat sold by cubic feet, even though it is much more expensive.

Burn stumps

❀ Pour leftover charcoal briquets, still burning from your backyard barbecue, on an unwanted tree stump. After several times, the stump will finally burn down below soil level.

Take care of tools

❀ Garden tools should be cleaned and the metal parts oiled after each use. Paint wooden handles before storing for the winter. With good care your tools should serve you well for many years.

❀ Pour some used oil into a bucket of sand and mix it with a spade. You now have a handy garden tool cleaner. Shove the tool into the oily sand a few times and wipe off with a rag.

❦ Mount a rural mailbox near or in your garden for a handy miniature tool shed. It is a good place to store trowels, garden shears, etc., to keep them handy yet dry.

❦ Keep the blade of your pruning saw from being damaged in storage. Use a piece of old garden hose, the same length as the blade. Carefully slit it lengthwise on one side, and slip it over the saw blade between uses.

❦ Keep your tool shed neat, and your rakes, hoes and other garden tools in order where you can find what you need without searching each time. Insert a screw eye into the end of the handle on each tool. Drive finishing nails in a row in the wall of the shed. Hang the tools on the nails.

Tools from jugs

❦ Make a scoop from a plastic jug. Cut off the handle and top in the correct shape, leaving the lid on.

❦ Cut off the bottom of a plastic jug and use the rest as a funnel for liquid fertilizer or other liquids. Remove the lid.

More handy tool ideas

❦ Mark your hoe handle in inches for a quick handy ruler to measure row width, distance between plants, etc. Either mark with paint or buy a roll of tape with measurements to stick onto the handle. Shellac to make it last longer.

❦ Cut both ends out of a large fruit-drink can and nail it to a post in the garden fence for a handy temporary tool rack. Slip the hoe and rake handles into the can. But don't leave them there when you leave the garden. Good tools deserve good care and a place out of the rain.

❦ An old metal tire rim makes an excellent holder for hanging your garden hose. Fasten it to the side of a building or on a post near the spigot. If you paint the rim the same color as the building, it won't be so noticeable. Hanging the hose over a nail eventually causes weak spots that may break. Leaving the hose lying on the ground makes it a nuisance when it is time to mow.

❦ A soda carton makes a handy carrier for small garden supplies and tools such as trowels, seed packets, and garden gloves.

❦ Recycle your old leaky garden hose by turning it into a soaker. Make small holes at regular intervals by driving finishing nails through the hose. Clamp the end shut or just leave a nozzle on the end, shut off.

❦ A child's wagon is a handy tool for a gardener. Use it to carry bags of fertilizer, buckets of water or soil, flats of plants, or whatever, to the garden or greenhouse.

❦ Make a sturdy trash sack to tie to your lawnmower handle for sticks, cans or other trash you may find as you mow. Use an old pair of worn-out jeans. Cut below the knee and sew at the cut to form a bag. Cut two pieces of twill tape 18 inches long for ties. Fold at the middle and sew them to the open end of the bag.

Watering is important

❦ A weekly deep watering is better than several light waterings. Light waterings encourage roots to grow upward rather than reaching down deeply into the soil as they should.

❦ If you have outdoor plants that need frequent watering, sink six- or eight-inch pots into the soil, up to the rims, near the plants. Pour water into the pots. The water will soak slowly into the soil through the pots' drain holes, and will be near the plants' roots. Water poured onto the soil often merely runs off, doing the plants little or no good.

❦ An old leaky bucket makes another excellent slow waterer for outdoor plants. Fill the bucket and set it near the plant. The water will leak slowly out of the bucket, soaking into the soil.

❦ During extremely dry weather, save dishwater and bathwater to use in the garden. Soap won't hurt the plants. It even helps get rid of insects. Pour at the base of the plants in the evening so the plant has all night to absorb it before the hot sun dries it out.

A weed to eat

❀ The common weed, lamb's-quarters, is good to eat. When you pull this weed from your garden, bring the leaves inside and add them to salads or cook them like spinach.

Two pretty wreaths to make

❀ Make a pretty wreath out of cornhusks. Start with a Styrofoam wreath base. Cut strips of cornhusks three inches wide and eight inches long. Fold in half crosswise and wire the ends together. Fasten to the foam base with thumbtacks, overlapping the folded part of one husk over the wire of the next, to hide the wires and tacks. If your base is narrow, make one row of husks. If it is wide, make two or more rows. Add a colorful bow. You can also add nuts, pinecones, or bittersweet for interest.

❀ Collect pinecones to make another pretty fall wreath. Cut a base for your wreath out of chicken wire, in the shape of a donut. Make it the size you want your wreath to be. Push the stem end of each pinecone through a hole in the chicken wire until it is held securely by its "petals." Keep adding cones, placing them as close together as possible, until the wire base is full. Add a bow, and possibly some nuts and dried pods for variety. Wire them on. Your wreath will be pretty for many years.

Index

MORE TIPS TO REMEMBER

MORE TIPS TO REMEMBER

MORE TIPS TO REMEMBER